Building Block Quilts 2

by Sara Nephew

Dedication

To all quilt shops, all quilt guilds, and the special shows and conferences that add excitement and support to a quilter's endeavors.

Acknowledgements

As always, I owe a debt of gratitude to the quilt artists who were willing to piece samples in 3-D: Annette Austin, Diane Coombs, Charisa Martin, Betty Parks, Mary Pierce, Laura Munson Reinstatler, Liz Thoman, and Lynn Williams.

Credits

Photography by Carl Murray
Graphics by Jean Streinz

Building Block Quilts

© Sara Nephew 1991

No part of this book may be reproduced by any electronic, mechanical, or other means, including informational storage or retrieval systems, for commercial use, without permission of the publisher.

Clearview Triangle

8311 180th St. S.E.
Snohomish, WA 98290

Library of Congress Card Number 89-82476
ISBN 0-9621172-2-6

Contents

4	Preface
4	Introduction
5	Special Techniques for 3-D Quilts
5	Choosing values instead of colors
6	Combining pattern sizes
7	Pattern distortion
8	3-D illusions
9	Tools
9	Rotary Cutting and Speed Piecing
10	Rules
10	Cutting directions
16	Sandwich piecing
17	Enlarging or shrinking patterns
18	The Quilts
20	Tumbling Tiles
22	Tumbling Bricks
24	Grandmother's Block Garden
26	Cliff-Dwellers
37	Strippy Quilt
40	Alphabet Blocks
42	Diamonds
44	Hollow Cube
46	Stairway
48	Endless Chains
50	Vistas
52	Through A Telescope
55	Wave
58	Stream
60	Space Crystal
63	Bibliography
63	Index

Preface

There has been an excellent response to *Building Block Quilts*, my previous book about isometric 3-D. And I am having too much fun to stop playing with 3-D illusions! There are more ideas that need to be worked out, more questions that need to be answered. There are more quilt designs to be pieced in beautiful fabrics. So, here is another collection of 3-D patterns from the 60° triangle.

Some of the patterns given here are simple to piece, and are fun to try in a variety of beautiful fabrics.

Others are more challenging, and carry the exciting 3-D illusions even further. For example, one of the possibilities of this method is to change the size of the pattern by changing the size of the basic triangle. Smaller and larger blocks are combined with intensive value shading in *Vistas* on pg. 30 and *Through A Telescope* on pg. 36 to produce interesting and impressive 3-D effects.

Another simple design approach to produce outstanding and innovative quilts is pattern distortion. Making a block stretched or flattened in the grid is shown all in one quilt pattern called *Wave* (see *Counterpoint* and *Frozen Rainbow*, two versions of this pattern, pg. 35), and in a larger version, *Stream*, pg. 34.

I hope you will find favorite quilts in this book. Perhaps you will want to try some fabrics that have been tempting you, or some new techniques that intrigue you.

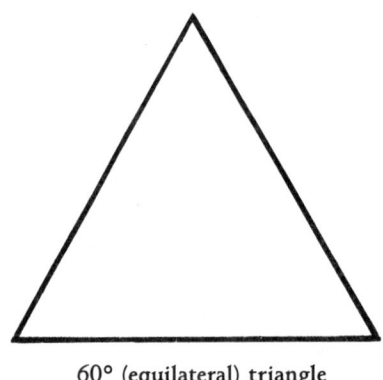

60° (equilateral) triangle

Introduction

Like the previous book, *Building Block Quilts*, this book is planned as a workbook. First some theory is given. Subjects covered include: tips for determining the value (darkness or lightness) of a fabric, constructing a value chart, combining different sizes of a pattern, pattern distortion, and a little review of isometric 3-D.

This information is followed by a description of the tools required, and the rotary cutting methods used in all the piecing. Some improvements have been added. The quilt patterns take up the rest of the book. They are organized generally with the easiest first, and the more challenging projects at the end of the section.

Even if you are familiar with the methods mentioned, it might be best to quickly read through the beginning sections of the book before beginning to piece a quilt. I hope you will enjoy these new dimensions in quilts!

Choosing Values Instead of Colors

Like riding a bicycle, seeing color as *value* is a skill that can be learned, and once learned is never really forgotten. (Value, the lightness or darkness of a color, is the key to the 3-D illusions achieved with the equilateral triangle). There are favorite methods for judging the value of a fabric. Looking through a piece of colored plastic (usually red) is one technique, and another approach sometimes mentioned is viewing a design through the wrong end of a pair of binoculars. Some quilters get extra use from their glasses by removing them.

My favorite way to determine value is to squint. Narrowing the eyes so less light comes in reduces the color element and increases perception of value. Squinting also allows the comparison of the lightness or darkness of busy or larger prints. The eye mixes the light and dark parts of these prints when we see them from a distance, or in a reduced light. This allows us to compare them, and to judge.

Begin to compare fabrics by laying one over the other. Choose a fabric you can be sure of, perhaps a definite light. Lay it out flat and put another fabric against it. Then lay it over the other fabric. Are they both light? Is one lighter than the other? When you have as many light fabrics as needed, begin to choose definite dark fabric(s) next. Last of all, choose mediums. Lay a medium fabric across the light fabric and then across the dark fabric. Try to find a medium that is exactly in between the light and the dark value, for the strongest 3-D effects.

For best results, work with fewer layers of material, as thick folds may cast a shadow and confuse the eye. Also avoid a lighter selvage or torn edge, folding distracting elements under.

A red sheet of plastic can help you judge values, but does not work well with some colors. Reds, yellows, and oranges are different from other hues. Just as insects see ultraviolet colors we can't perceive, our eyes react in a unique way to all "warm" colors. We may speculate that these are the colors of danger, markings used by poisonous reptiles and insects, the colors of fire. These colors glow to our eyes and this glow makes them lighter in value. These colors can add life and vibrance to a quilt, especially if they are set off by cooler tones. (See *Space Crystal*, pg. 33)

An excellent technique to use when working with a large selection of fabrics is to construct a value chart. A small piece (perhaps 1" x 4") is cut from each fabric that might be used in a quilt. Be sure to remove any selvage. Then arrange these swatches in order from light to dark. Squinting at this layout often reveals a bar of light or dark in the row, showing that a particular fabric is out of place. When the swatches are laid out to your satisfaction, use a glue stick or fabric glue to put the grouping onto a piece of light cardboard (like a file folder). Wipe off the excess glue with a damp cloth, and put the chart under books and/or a cutting board to dry flat.

This value chart is now a tool for choosing the light, medium, and dark fabrics for any block, for finding a fabric even though cutting and piecing has produced a jumbled and unrecognizable pile of materials, or for adding additional choices from the large selection at your favorite quilt shop. It also shows the fabric cut up, instead of in a large piece. The fabric chart can help give the quilter a feeling of being in control.

A value chart is not necessary for most of the quilt patterns in this book, but a few of them require at least 9 different values to achieve the best 3-D effects. And even the simplest projects can be made into works of art by skillful control of a more complex range of values.

When designs emphasize value, often the weaknesses of a quilter's fabric collection begin to show up. Some quilters, without knowing it, have concentrated on medium colors without collecting any light or dark fabrics. Others have all light and dark, with few mediums. This may require some purchases to supply the missing range of colors. Future quilts will gain added radiance, both from an expanded fabric library and from the knowledge acquired by working with 3-D quilts.

Value Chart on Cardboard

Combining Pattern Sizes

These rotary cutting methods allow the quilter to change the size or scale of a pattern by simply changing the size of the basic triangle. For example, you could surround a center of large blocks with a border of the same pattern in miniature, or combine different sizes of the same pattern to achieve an increased illusion of depth.

The first aim might be to have the various sections of a quilt fit easily together. Finished size of a large triangle should equal the finished size of multiple small triangles. Then they will sew together easily, with ending seams coming out even. Begin with finished sizes that fit together, and add seam allowances. Work with the perpendicular height of the 60° triangle.

For example, two 1½" triangles combine to equal a 3" triangle. Add seam allowances to each size. A triangle loses ¾" in height when seams are taken. Adding ¾" to both the large and small size results in two cut sizes: 1½" + ¾" = 2¼" and 3" + ¾" = 3¾". These are two basic triangle sizes that will seam together neatly. You can also choose other sizes.

A size in-between might be a smooth transition to increase a 3-D illusion. This will not always be a size that matches the other two. Strips of background fabric can be used to make sections fit each other, or perhaps simply trimming the in-between section at the outside edge of the quilt would be a design solution.

More intensive shading added to a combination of sizes may increase the illusion of depth. Each section of the pattern needs light, medium, and dark fabrics. If the largest pattern is also the lightest light, medium, dark combination it will look closer. If the smallest pattern is the darkest light, medium, dark combination it will look farther away. So at least 9 different values need to be found in fabric; three for light 3-D, three for medium 3-D, three for dark 3-D. (I have a theory that perhaps five values would be sufficient to achieve an effect of graded shading—see the chart on the right—but somehow the enjoyment of finding fabrics for a project always has resulted in a considerably larger selection than the minimum).

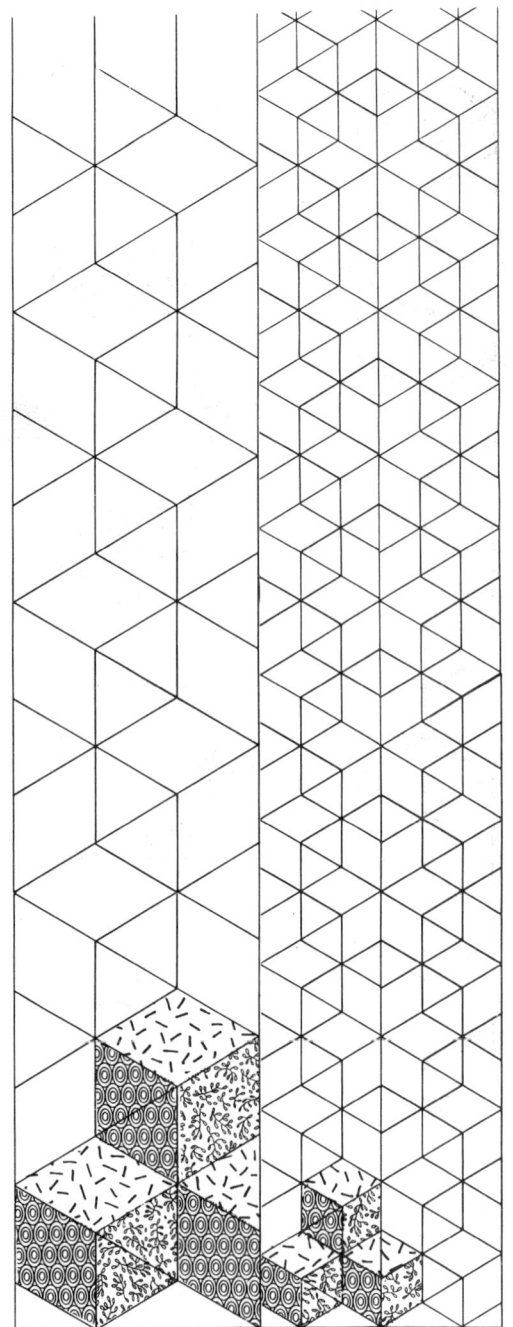

Different-sized Blocks

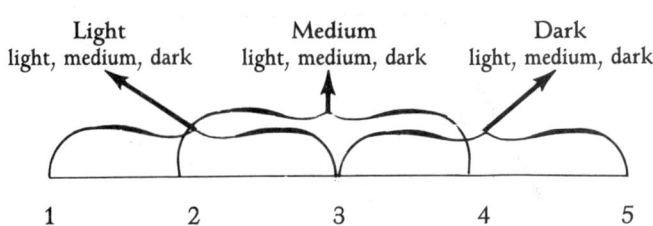

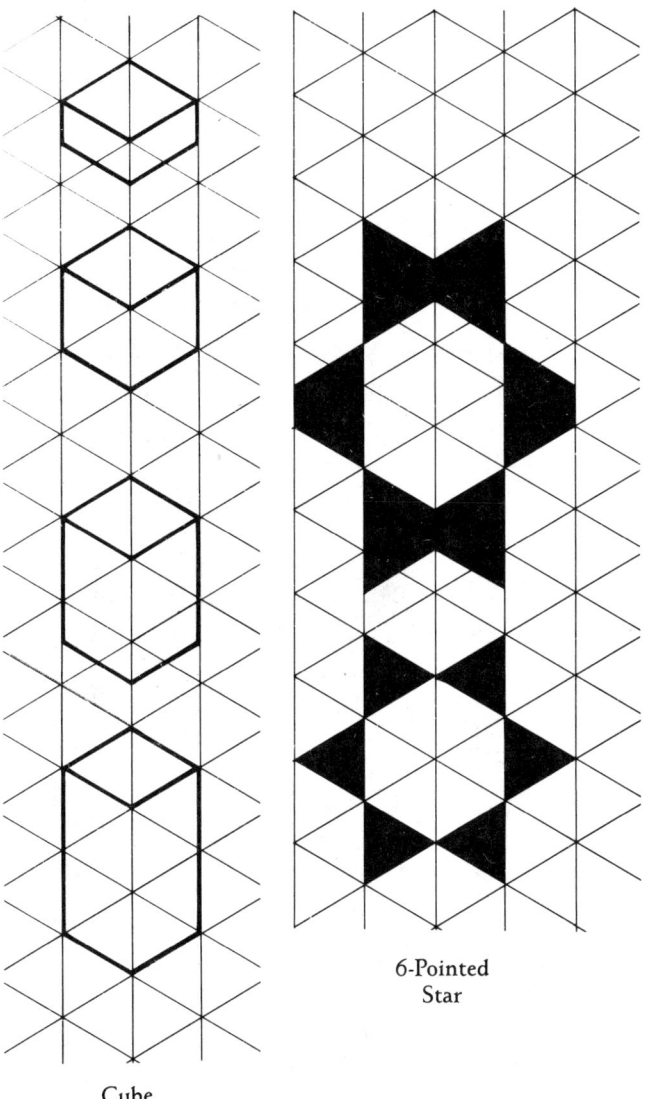

Cube

6-Pointed Star

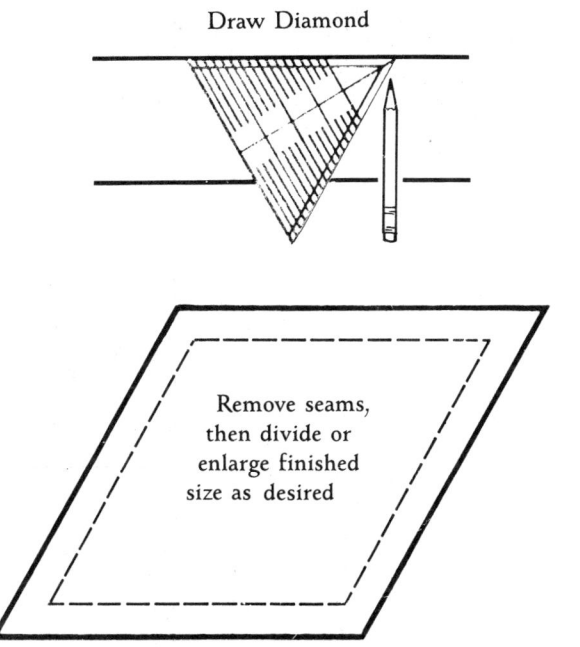

Draw Diamond

Remove seams, then divide or enlarge finished size as desired

Pattern Distortion

Another design approach to producing outstanding and innovative quilts is pattern distortion. Some quilters have redrafted traditional blocks, elongating or widening them in the edges or center of the quilt design. This may seem to make the center of the quilt bulge and the edges recede. More templates for the different shaped squares are then needed.

Elongating or shortening designs on isometric graph paper produces easy new patterns as well as fun and exciting illusions. *Tumbling Tiles* on pg. 29 is a flattened *Tumbling Blocks* pattern. *Tumbling Bricks* on pg. 32 is an elongated block, very easy and elegant to piece. Different lengths of blocks are combined in *Wave*, pg. 55. *Tumbling Tiles* and *Tumbling Bricks* in the *Wave* pattern are drawn by: shortening a diamond to half a diamond on the vertical grid, and lengthening a diamond to 1½ and 2 times as long as the basic diamond on the vertical grid. This vertical distortion produces a number of possible illusions in one quilt, as shown by the quilt examples in color on pg. 35. First, the illusion of the cube catches attention, then the flattened tiles curve closer or farther away, balancing the elongated bricks. Last, the illusion of a curved line is produced along the diagonal row of cubes, even though only straight seams are sewed.

These patterns can be easily cut without templates following the rules given in the cutting directions, or using the *Table of Common Shapes* on pg. 18. If necessary, some simple math will solve any additional problems. For example, to determine the strip width and line on the triangle for the *Tumbling Tile* piece in *Wave*, use the cutting directions, the Clearview Triangle, and a sharp pencil to draw the standard diamond for your pattern (2¾″ by 2¾″ if the basic triangle is 3″). Then remove seam allowances by drawing lines ¼″ inside the outside edges. Divide the remaining shape in half (1⅛″) and add seam allowances back on. This gives the strip width to cut. Then lay the Clearview Triangle over the drawing to see what line on the triangle to cut this long diamond on. The piece is cut at 2¾″ from a 1⅝″ strip—all that you need to know. The same method is used for the long diamond that is 1½ times a basic diamond, and the other long diamond is pictured in the *Table of Common Shapes*, so no math is necessary.

These designs may be colored in a number of different ways, emphasizing different illusions. For this reason, when working with any distorted design a few copies of the design grid may need to be colored in different ways to see what illusion possibilities can be found. Diagrams that can be copied and colored are given for each quilt pattern in this book.

3-D Illusions

A short review of the theory of isometric 3-D might be helpful, especially if you don't have the previous book. The 3-D illusions in this book are based on the 60° triangle. The angles used in this kind of drawing are 60°, 30°, and 120°. When these angles and shapes are shaded, our eye sees objects in three dimensions. This is called *isometric* drawing. (The word is from the Greek and means "equal measure," referring to the 3 equal sides and 3 equal angles of the 60° triangle). Artists like M.C. Escher and Victor Vasarely have used these angles and illusions to create challenging and inspirational works of art.

On a much simpler level, the quilter can begin with equilateral graph paper, choose outlines, add shading and create a 3-D illusion quilt design. At right are some examples of shading outlines to create a 3-D shape.

You may wish to repeat one shape or combine many shapes in one quilt. Artistic decisions must always be made about balance, rhythm, etc., to achieve an attractive pattern. Other approaches include varying and combining the size of the figures, and adding a background against which the 3-D shapes float. Many exciting quilts wait to be designed.

Planning how to piece the quilt can often be easy, using the cutting rules in this book, the *Table of Common Shapes*, and perhaps some simple math.

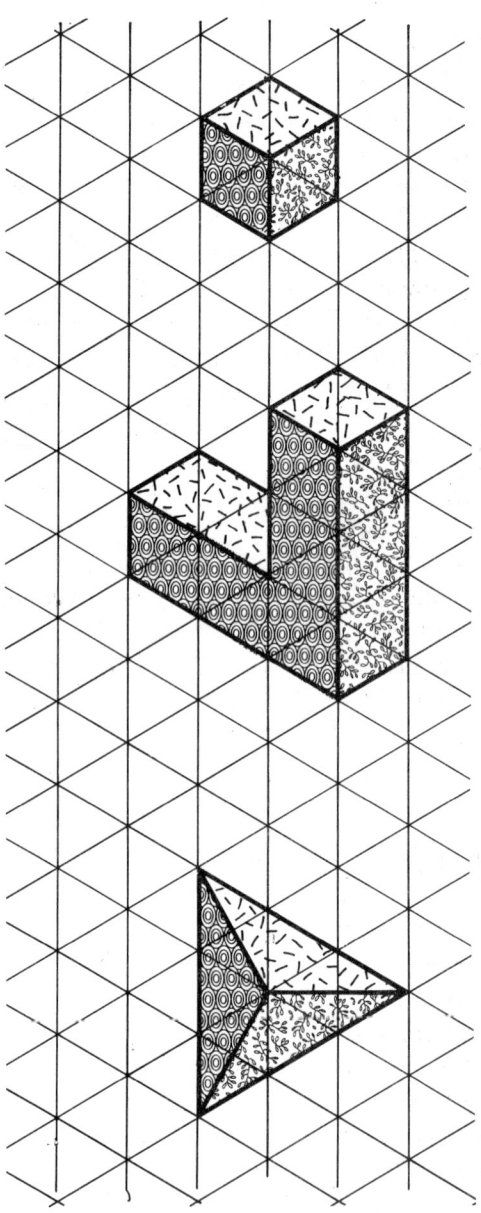

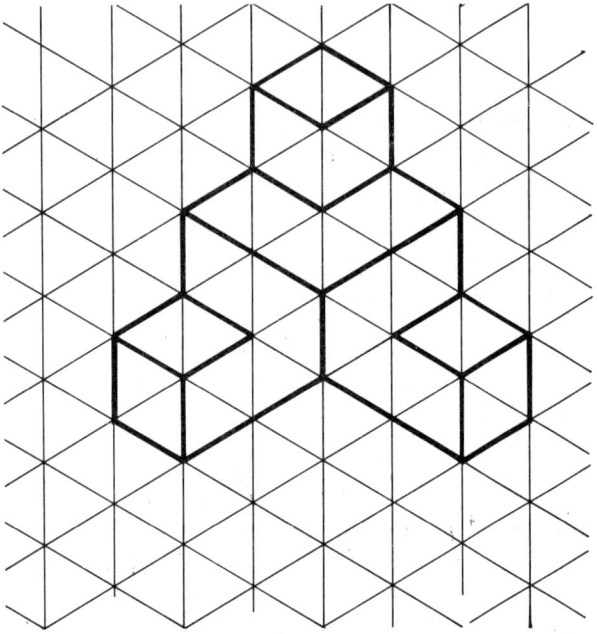

You can even draw "impossible" shapes!

Page eight — *Building Block Quilts 2*

Tools

Two key tools go a long way in saving time when making three-sided quilts. The **Clearview Triangle** makes rotary cutting and accurate piecing of 60° triangles, 60° diamonds, hexagons, etc., fast and easy. The Triangles comes in three sizes. The **Clearview Half-Diamond** is designed especially for rotary cutting speed-pieced 60° diamonds divided lengthwise into two different fabrics. It also speeds the cutting of other shapes. These tools are made from 1/8" acrylic, for use with a rotary cutter. (See page 64 for ordering information).

Besides Clearview Triangles, required tools are: a rotary cutter, a cutting mat, and a clear, straight ruler like the Salem Rule or Omnigrid (for cutting strips). A large rotary cutter is preferred, since it saves muscle strain, cuts faster, and tends to stay on a straight line. I also like a ruler that measures 6"×12" for my strip cutting method (see page 10). The shorter rule is less likely to move during cutting.

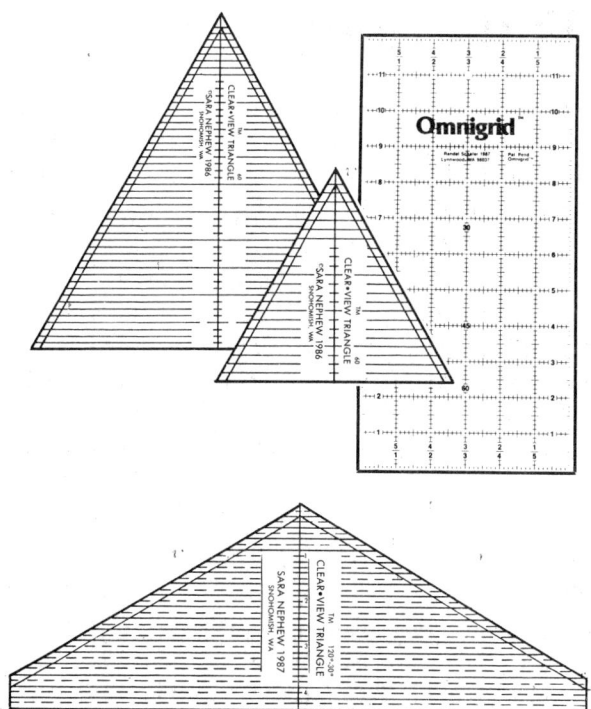

Rotary Cutting and Speed Piecing

For a little while, please set aside all thoughts of seam allowances, cardboard templates, and fabric as yardage. Consider only:
1. A strip of fabric;
2. A plastic 60° triangle with a ruled line on the perpendicular.

Every technique in this book is based on these 2 elements. The triangle is laid over the strip in various ways, and a rotary cutter is used along the edges of the triangle to cut off portions of the fabric strip.

Nothing in this book is difficult to do as long as the triangle and the strip are kept in mind. The strip may be changed by making it wider or narrower, or by sewing it to another strip before doing any cutting. The triangle may be changed by making it larger or smaller, or by changing it from a 60° (equilateral) triangle to a 120° half-diamond.

By working just with these elements, **many** shapes can be cut in whatever size desired. These shapes will all fit together to form a design, a quilt top.

After doing a large number of these quilts, I have found that it is not necessary to calculate all measurements each time a new design is cut and pieced. Instead, knowledge of a few basic rules often makes the next step automatic.

The following section first lists the rules and then describes the methods for cutting various shapes, emphasizing the rule for each operation. Please read through the whole section before beginning to piece any of the patterns in this book. The index at the back of the book offers easy access so you can review cutting methods while piecing a particular pattern.

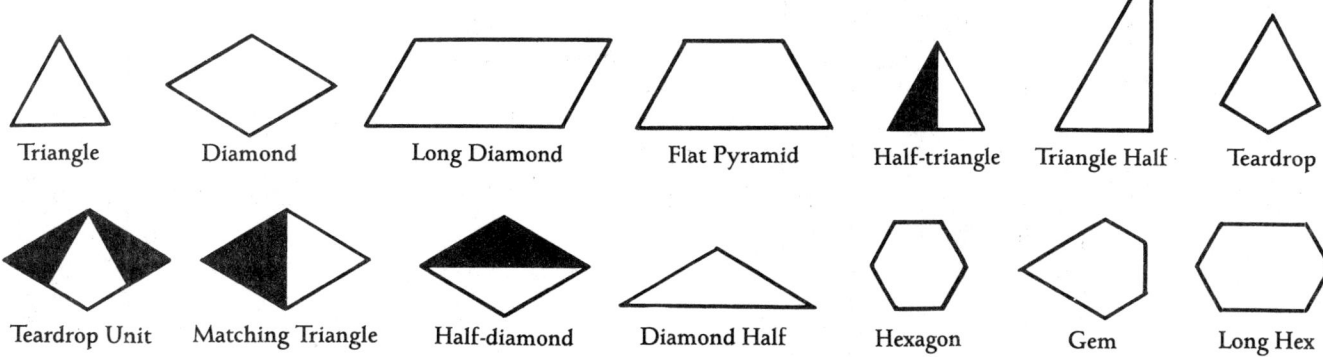

Building Block Quilts 2 — Page nine

* Rules

1. Before beginning to cut and piece a design, a **triangle size** is chosen to determine the scale of the design. The triangle size is the perpendicular measurement. A 3" triangle measures 3" from tip to base. (A **triangle size** is given for each pattern in the book).
2. A triangle is cut from a strip whose width is the same as the height of the triangle's perpendicular.
3. Diamonds, long diamonds, and flat pyramids are cut from a strip ¼" narrower than the strip a triangle is cut from.
4. Half-triangles, triangle halves and teardrops are cut from a strip ½" wider than the strip a triangle is cut from.
5. To draft a hexagon, use a triangle measuring ½" less than the **triangle size** chosen.
6. A hexagon is cut from a strip whose width is twice the perpendicular of the triangle used to draft the hexagon. (See hexagon table page 14)

* All of the rules and measurements in this book apply if a ¼" seam is taken.

Cutting Strips

The first step in cutting any shape is cutting strips. All fabric should be prewashed. 100% cotton is preferred.

1. Fold fabric selvage to selvage and press. If pressing from the selvage to the fold produces wrinkles, move the top layer of fabric left or right keeping selvages parallel, until wrinkles disappear.
2. Bring fold to selvage (folding again) and press.
3. Use the wide ruler as a right angle guide, or line up the selvages with the edge of the mat, and the ruler with the mat edge perpendicular to the selvage. Cut off the ragged or irregular edges of the fabric.
4. Cut the strip width required, using the newly cut fabric edge as a guide.
5. Open the strip. It should be straight, not zig zag, if you had the ruler at right angles to the selvages and folds. Adjust the ruler slightly if necessary and trim fabric edges slightly before cutting the next strip.

Cutting Directions

The cutting directions given in this book are essentially the same as those in the previous books, STARS AND FLOWERS and BUILDING BLOCK QUILTS. A few changes and improvements have been made. Also, some of the shapes that can be cut are not needed in these patterns; but I have left the cutting directions in here for those who may devise a 3-D design requiring these shapes.

To cut triangles:

Rule: A triangle is cut from a strip whose width is the same as the height of the triangles' perpendicular. Example: A 3" triangle is cut from a strip 3" wide.

1. Position the tip of the Clearview Triangle at one edge of the strip, and the 3" ruled line at the other edge of the strip.
2. Rotary cut along the 2 sides of the triangle. Move the Clearview Triangle along the same edge (do not flip it to the other side of the fabric strip) for the next cut, lining up the cut point of the fabric strip with the 3" line on the plastic triangle. Check to be sure the strip edge is right along the ruled line.
3. Cut along both sides of the triangle. (Strips may be stacked up to 8 thicknesses and all cut at once.)

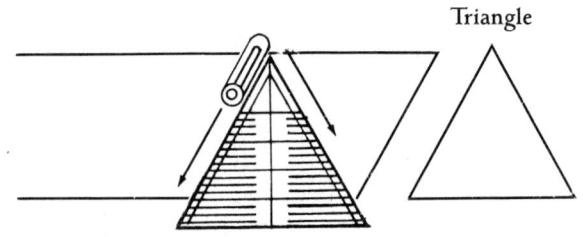

Diamond

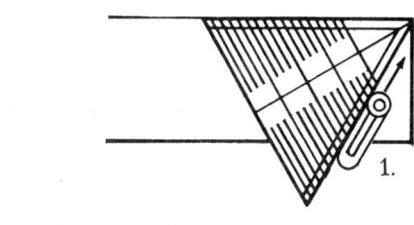

To cut diamonds:

Rule: Diamonds, long diamonds and flat pyramids are cut from a strip ¼" narrower than the strip a triangle is cut from.

1. Position the Clearview Triangle with one side along one edge of the strip. Strip should be ¼" narrower than the triangle size chosen for the design. Cut the end of the strip to a 60° angle.

2. Reposition the Clearview Triangle so the tip is at one edge of the strip and a ruled line is along the other edge. (The same position as is used to cut triangles, except the strip is ¼" narrower.)

3. Rotary cut **only** along the side opposite the first cut.

4. Keep moving the tool along the same side of the strip, lining up the cut edge and the side of the tool as shown. Always cut the side opposite the first cut. (Strips may be stacked up to 8 thicknesses and all cut at once.)

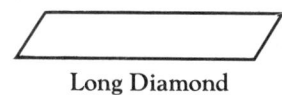
Long Diamond

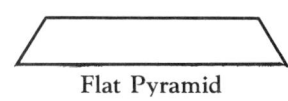
Flat Pyramid

To cut long diamonds and flat pyramids:

Rule: Diamonds, long diamonds and flat pyramids are cut from a strip ¼" narrower than the strip a triangle is cut from.

Method #1
Trim one end of the strip to a 60° angle. Sew long side of the strip to the piece desired. Trim the other end to the correct angle.

Method #2 (Long Diamond)
1. Trim one end of the strip to a 60° angle.
2. Place the Clearview Triangle over the fabric strip, with a 60° fabric triangle extending from under the tool, and the cut edge lined up at the tool edge. Set the bottom edge of the strip at the measurement given in the pattern, or according to the TABLE OF COMMON SHAPES (pg. 18). Cut the side opposite the first cut.

Method #3 (Flat Pyramid)
Place the Clearview Triangle over the fabric strip, lining up one edge of the strip at the measurement given in the pattern, or according to the TABLE OF COMMON SHAPES (pg. 18). Cut each side of the strip.

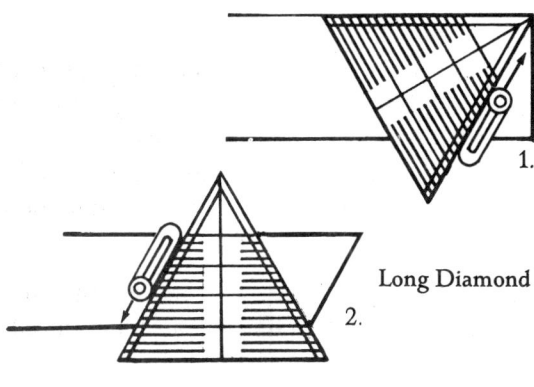

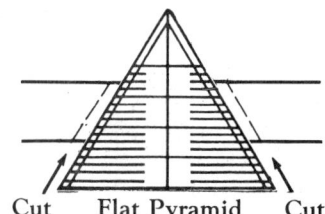

Note: care must be taken when cutting long diamonds, as they do have a reverse of their shape. Check carefully to be sure you are cutting them in the direction required by the pattern. If you don't need both the long diamond and its reverse, keep fabric right sides up. Try cutting just one first, to be sure it's right.

To cut a triangle half:

Rule: Half-triangles, triangle halves, and teardrops are cut from a strip ½" wider than the strip a triangle is cut from.

Method #1
1. Cut triangles from a strip ½" wider than the triangle size chosen for the design.
2. Bisect these triangles on the perpendicular. Line up the side of the fabric triangle with the perpendicular line of the Clearview Triangle, then cut the fabric triangle in half along the ruler edge.

Method #2
1. Cut a rectangle the height needed for the triangle half and half the width of that triangle's base (measure with a ruler). Then bisect this rectangle from corner to corner diagonally. (This will produce 2 halves the same, rather than a left and a right. Lay the ruler from corner to corner to check and see if this is the shape needed. If not, lay it along the other 2 corners.)

To cut diamond half:

Method #1
Use the Clearview Half-Diamond to rotary cut 120° triangles from the proper width strip. (See the table of measurements for half diamonds on page 16.)

Method #2
1. Line up center line of tool with edge of fabric strip cut at the width required. (See the table of measurements for half diamonds on page 16.)

2. Flip tool, line up center line with strip edge and previous cut at edge of tool. Cut other 30° angle.

Finding the Strip Width for a Half-Diamond or diamond half

(See the table of measurements for half diamonds on page 16.)

Use a fine-tipped pen or sharp pencil and slant it toward the ruler.

1. Using the plastic template, draw your triangle

2. Mark and draw the perpendicular line, extending it below your triangle's perpendicular.

3. Reverse the plastic template. Line it up along the extended perpendicular line, with the base line of the drawn triangle exactly under the same lines less ½"on the plastic template (3½" for a 4" triangle.)

4. Draw one side.

5. Add ¼" seam allowance to the perpendicular line, extending sides to meet.

Page twelve — *Building Block Quilts 2*

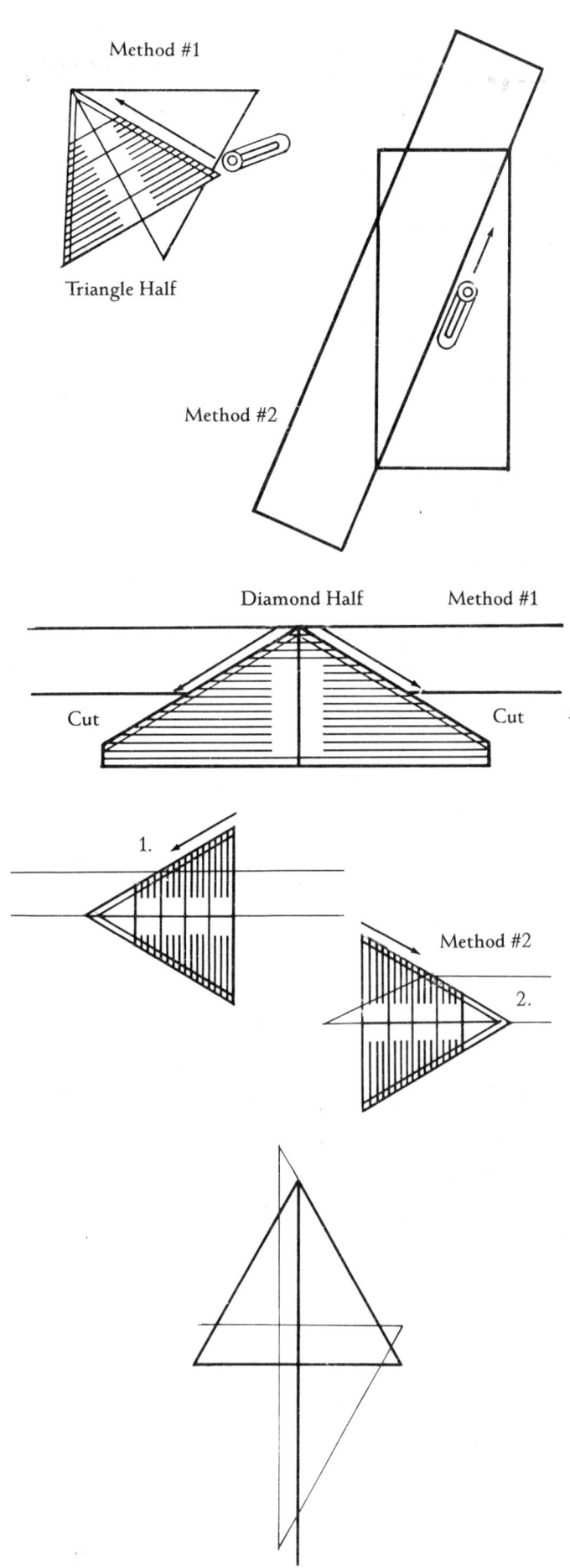

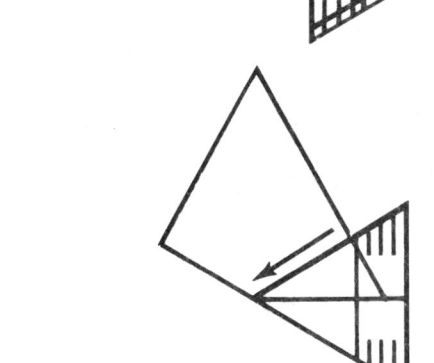

Cut Teardrop Method #1

Method #2

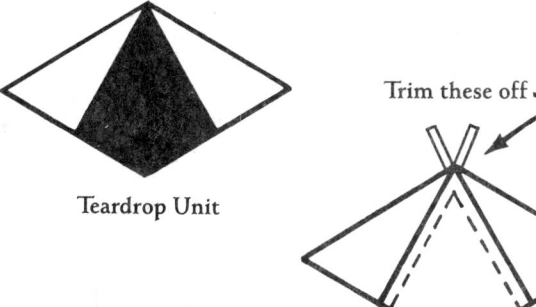

Teardrop Unit

Trim these off

To cut a teardrop:

Rule: Half-triangles, triangle halves, and teardrops are cut from strips ½" wider than the strip a triangle is cut from.

Method #1

1. Cut triangles from a strip ½" wider than the **triangle size** required.

2. Position Clearview Half-Diamond on triangle so its tip is opposite triangle tip. Line up the triangle point with the perpendicular of the Half-Diamond and line the triangle sides up evenly with one of the rulings, as shown. Then use rotary cutter to cut the base of the teardrop.

Method #2

1. Cut triangles as #1 above.

2. Measure the base of these triangles and find the center or half measurement.

3. Lay the perpendicular of the Clearview Triangle along the base of the fabric triangle, with the point at center. Rotary cut this wedge off. Reverse the template and cut off the other base corner.

Teardrop Unit

A teardrop unit, made from 1 teardrop shape and 2 triangle halves, is very useful. Seam one triangle half on each side of the teardrop to make a diamond-shaped unit. I line these pieces up for seaming at the bottom, not the top. Press each seam. Trim off the little seam ears to finish. This piece requires careful attention, both in cutting and seaming. If too small, narrower seam width is the solution.

Drafting Hexagons With the Clearview Triangle

To draft an accurate hexagon using the Clearview Triangle, two methods can be used. For method one:

1. Draw two sides of the triangle, marking the desired base line.

2. Extend these lines with a ruler.

3. Position the template along one line and draw the third intersecting line. Extend this line also.

4. Use a compass to draw a circle the marked distance along the lines. (Set the point in the center of the intersecting lines.)

5. Connect the lines at the compass markings.

Method two eliminates the compass. Simply mark the triangle base along each line and connect the marks. Either way, these hexagons include seam allowance.

(It is usually not necessary to actually draft the hexagon.)

Two rules apply

Rule: To draft a hexagon, use a triangle measuring ½" less than the **triangle size** chosen.

Rule: A hexagon is cut from a strip whose width is twice the perpendicular of the triangle used to draft the hexagon.

SEE TABLE BELOW

Example: **3" triangle size**—draft the hexagon from 2½" triangles.

2½"+2½"=5" strip. This will yield a hexagon that a 3" triangle will sew on to.

To cut a hexagon:

1. Cut a fabric strip according to the pattern directions, or according to the hexagon table below.

2. Cut 60° diamonds from the strip. (See "to cut diamonds", pg. 11).

3. From each end of the diamonds, cut a triangle whose size is ½ of the strip width. Example: 5" strip means a 2½" triangle must be removed from each end of each diamond.

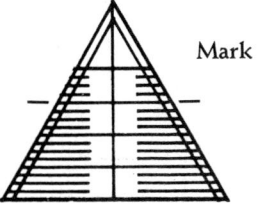
Mark

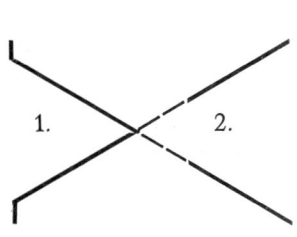
1.   2.

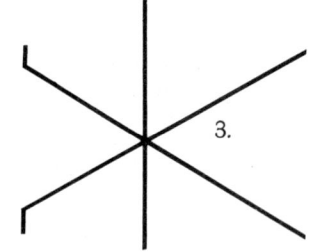
3.

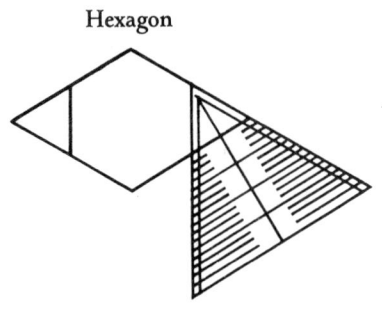
Hexagon

HEXAGON TABLE

Triangle size	Strip to cut	Cut off triangle
1"	1"	½"
2"	3"	1½"
3"	5"	2½"
4"	7"	3½"
5"	9"	4½"
6"	11"	5½"

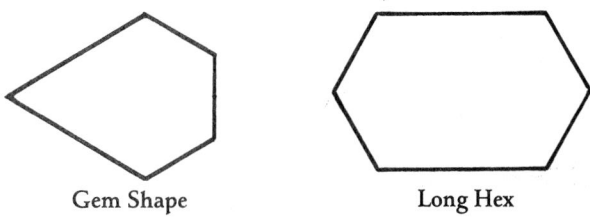

Gem Shape — Long Hex

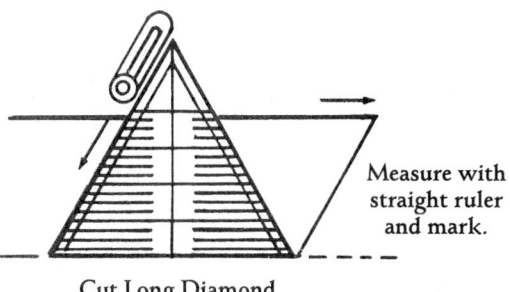

Cut Long Diamond — Measure with straight ruler and mark.

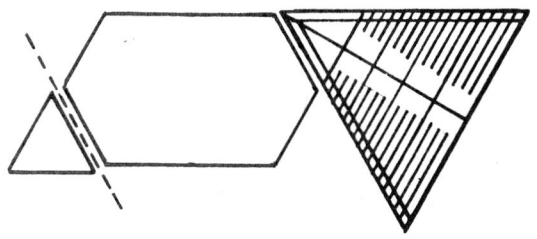

To cut a gem shape

Instead of cutting a hexagon from the diamond, cut only one point off, leaving this shape.

To cut a long hex

1. Cut a strip width according to the HEXAGON TABLE.

2. Cut a long diamond (see pg. 11). The length of the long side is:

Triangle Size	Side Length
2″	4¼″
3″	7¼″
4″	10¼″
5″	13¼″
6″	16¼″

Cut one side, make a pencil mark at the other side, and cut to a 60° angle at this pencil mark.

3. From each end of the long diamond, cut a triangle whose size is ½ of the strip width. (Same as **cutting a hexagon,** page 14.)

(The long hex is not used in any of the patterns given in this book, but could be used in many designs. Example shown.)

Piecing Hints

All my piecing is done with ¼″ seams. Even if the presser foot on your sewing machine features this ¼″ for you, it is a good idea to measure the seams occasionally until you are confident of accuracy. Check to be sure the seam is **just inside** the ¼″ line rather than right on it.

When many seams intersect at one point, pinch the center where the seams cross, open the fabric to see how the seams are meeting and adjust as necessary. Pin to hold the fabric for seaming.

A few tips about trimming seams are included in the cutting instructions. I trim in a number of places to reduce bulk as the quilt top is pieced. Be careful not to trim too much off before the next step, however, as the little points that stick out help align the parts for accurate sewing. Experience helps. The mild bias of the triangles also aids in lining up seams. Pull a little if necessary. All seams are pressed to one side to make quilting easier.

Sandwich Piecing

To sandwich piece matching triangle units (sandwich piecing uses 2 strips of fabric):
1. Cut strips of fabric the width of the triangle size. Two different fabrics are used, usually one light and one dark. Seam these strips right sides together with a ¼" seam down both the right and the left side of the pair of strips. Position the Clearview Triangle so the tip is at one edge of the strips, and the ruled line for the correct size triangle at the other edge. Rotary cut on both sides of the tool. (Same as cutting triangles.)
2. Pull the tips of the seamed triangles apart and press open.

To sandwich piece half-diamond units
1. Cut strips of fabric whose width equals the perpendicular measurement of one-half the unit desired, including seam allowance, or according to the measurements given in the half-diamond table below. Two different fabrics are used, usually one light and one dark.
2. Sew light and dark strips right sides together with a ¼" seam allowance down each side.
3. Using a Clearview Half-Diamond and a rotary cutter, cut triangles from the seamed strips. Line up the ruler tip at one seamed edge, and the desired line on the ruler at the other edge, and cut as for triangles.
4. Use a seam ripper to cut one stitch at the seamed tip of the fabric 120° triangles.
5. Pull the tips of the seamed triangles apart and press open, pressing across the width of the diamond and pulling the top and bottom out straight while pressing.
6. Trim off the little seam ears as shown.

HALF-DIAMOND TABLE

Triangle Size	Strip Width
2"	1¼"
3"	1⅞"
4"	2⅜"

Triangle Size	Strip Width
5"	3"
6"	3½"

To sandwich piece half-triangle units:
Rule: Half-triangles, triangle halves, and teardrops are cut from a strip ½" wider than the strip a triangle is cut from.
Note: this rule is being applied in a different way in these new IMPROVED sandwich piecing directions.

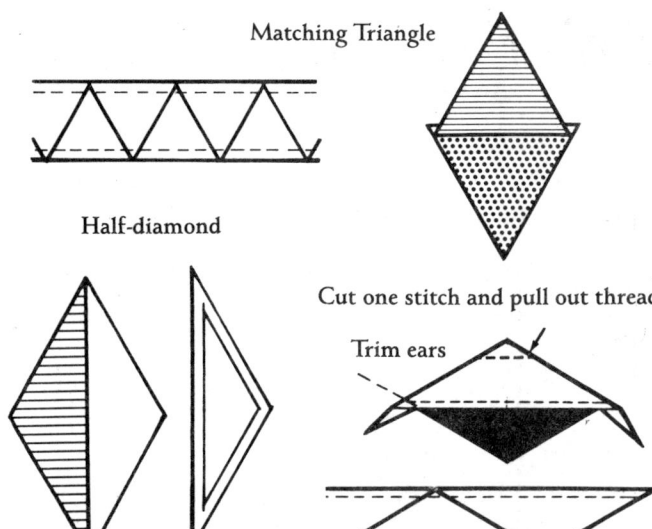

1. Cut two fabric strips according to the table below, or measure ½ the base of a triangle ½" bigger than the triangle you are working with. (design triangle)
2. Sew light and dark strips right sides together with a ¼" seam allowance down each side.
3. Cut these strips into sections according to the table below or ½" bigger than the triangle you are working with.
4. Bisect sections diagonally by lining up center line of the Clearview Triangle along one edge, and new base line at bottom. Turn remaining section part to other edge and check accuracy. This produces 2 left or 2 right half-triangles. To obtain the other kind, flip section over so other fabric is up.

Triangle Size	Strip Width	Cut into Sections
2"	1⁷⁄₁₆"	2½"
3"	2"	3½"
4"	2⅝"	4½"
5"	3⅜"	5½"
6"	3¾"	6½"

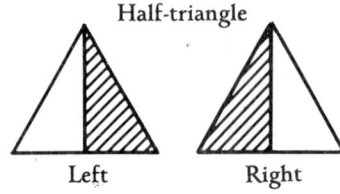

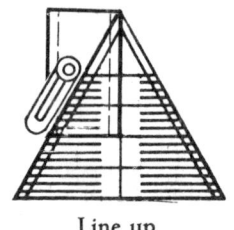

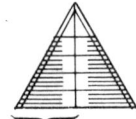

Measure from center to edge at new triangle measurement after applying rule #4
ext. 3" triangle becomes 3½"

Enlarging or Shrinking a Pattern

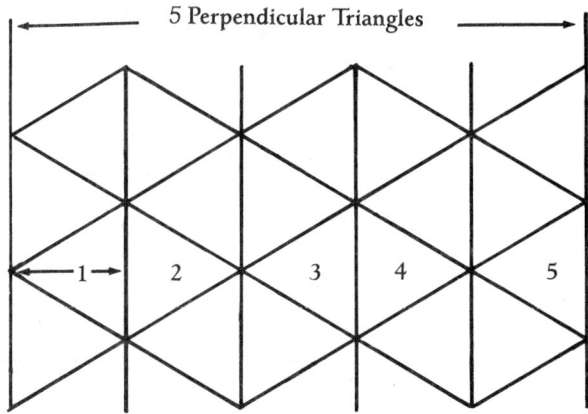

3" Design Triangle

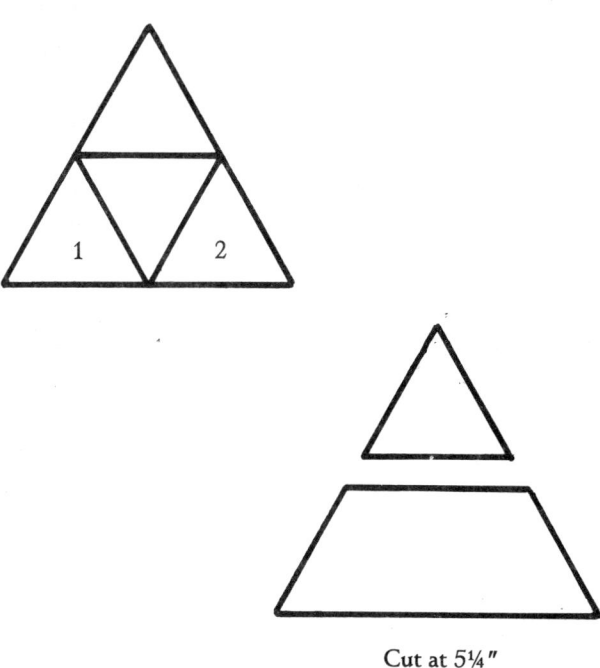

Cut at 5¼"

Cut at 5"

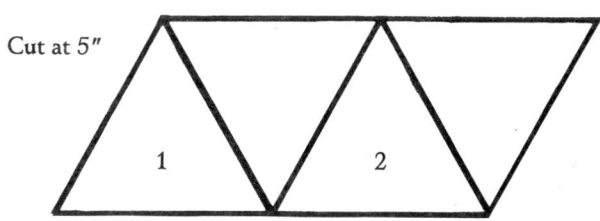

It's fun to try substituting a different **triangle size** when piecing a particular quilt design. Following are instructions on how to do a rough estimate of how altering triangle size will change the size of the quilt. (To calculate new dimensions exactly, see pg. 19).

The perpendicular triangle measurement is easy to figure. Just subtract ¾" from the triangle size chosen to obtain "finished" height and multiply by the number of triangles perpendicular across the grid of the quilt design. (If this is not easily seen, sketch the design on graph paper.)

By comparing the new measurement with the original, you can then estimate the other dimension of the quilt. Let's use TUMBLING BRICKS (pg. 22).

The body of the quilt, without borders, has 18 perpendicular triangles across the width. Using a 3" triangle size, the quilt width is 40½" (2¼"×18) without borders. Changing to a 2" triangle size results in a width of 22½" (1¼"×18) without borders, almost ½ the width of the larger quilt. Half the width and ½ the length would mean a quilt about ¼ the size. In this quilt, the change would be from a baby quilt to a doll quilt by reducing one triangle size.

To substitute a new triangle size follow the RULES and CUTTING DIRECTIONS for all the standard pieces. For larger pieces, or for flat pyramids, etc. the following information and table will be helpful. Use this information to change the size of shapes or to find the size of a shape in an original design.

When a shape is on graph paper, it can be analyzed and its size determined using simple math. Count the rows in the shape.

Example: This shape is composed of a triangle and a flat pyramid. Triangle cut from 3" strip, loses ¼" seam when sewed to flat pyramid. Flat pyramid cut from 2¾" strip, loses ¼" seam when sewed to triangle.

Result: 2¾" triangle height + 2½" flat pyramid height so shape is cut at 5¼" line on Clearview Triangle. (All the math in this example is based on a 3" triangle size).

The long diamond is a special case. It uses the same measurement as the other shapes, minus ¼".

EX. Table of common shapes shows 2 triangles on base of shape. 3" triangle size-cut at 5¼" on the Clearview Triangle. A long diamond is needed with 2 triangles on the bottom side. Cut at 5" on the Clearview Triangle–¼" less than the table measurement for the triangle or flat pyramid.

Common Shapes

Design Triangle size	Use this base line on the Clearview Triangle
2″	3¼″
3″	5¼″
4″	7¼″
5″	9¼″
6″	11¼″

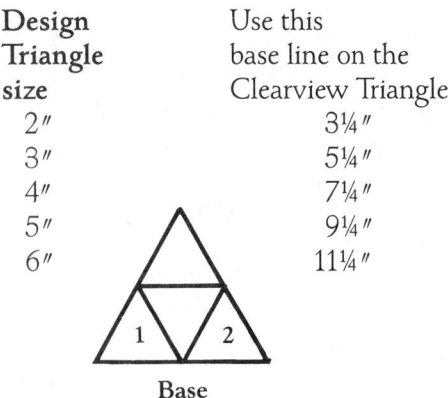

Design Triangle size	Use this base line on the Clearview Triangle
2″	4½″
3″	7½″
4″	10½″
5″	13½″
6″	16½″

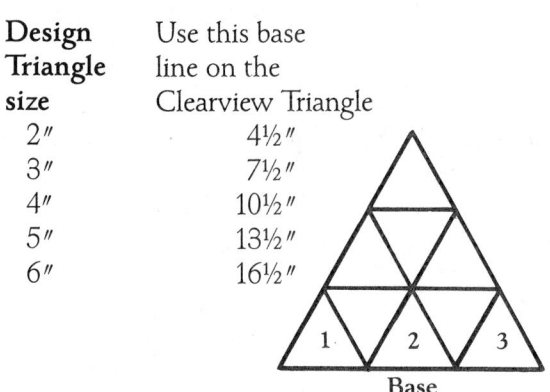

Design Triangle size	Use this base line on the Clearview Triangle
2″	5¾″
3″	9¾″
4″	13¾″
5″	17¾″
6″	21¾″

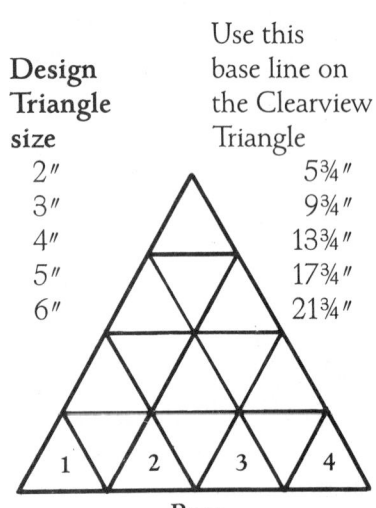

Flat Pyramid

Design Triangle size		Use this base line on the Clearview Triangle
2″	3¼″	
3″	5¼″	
4″	7¼″	
5″	9¼″	
6″	11¼″	

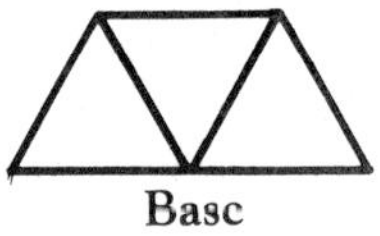

Flat Pyramid

Design Triangle size	Use this base line on the Clearview Triangle
2″	4½″
3″	7½″
4″	10½″
5″	13½″
6″	16½″

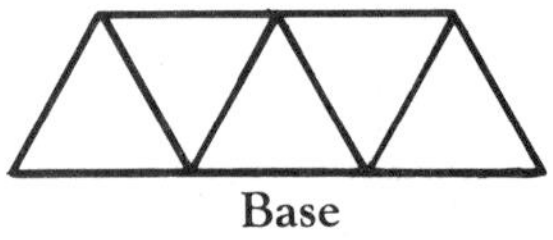

Long Diamond

Design Triangle size	Use this base line on the Clearview Triangle
2″	3″
3″	5″
4″	7″
5″	9″
6″	11″

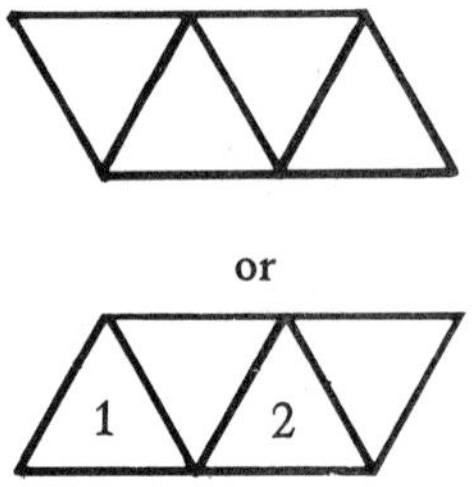

Example: To change a 2″ triangle pattern to a 3″ pattern, follow the tables above and when the dimension called for is 3¼″, subsitute 5¼″; when the dimension called for is 5¾″, substitute 9¾″; etc.

The Quilts

How to Use These Diagrams

These quilt diagrams depict each design by value, showing only light, medium, dark, and background shades. Substitute your own fabric in these values, whether plaid, flowered, or plain-colored. Value (lightness or darkness of shading) is the most important consideration.

To follow the cutting directions given for each quilt or block, please note: often cutting directions are given completely, including:
1. strip width, and
2. line used on Clearview Triangle.

If these are not both included, then a rule applies. The rules are listed on pg. 10 and with each cutting method described. (See index pg. 63 to find page numbers for all cutting directions.)

For example: if directions say, "Cut a flat pyramid from a 2¾" strip at 9¾"," strip width is given, and the line on the triangle is given. (The person cutting, if unfamiliar with the methods, may still need to review pg. 11 to see how to cut a flat pyramid.)

The next direction may say: "Cut a flat pyramid at 7½"." Strip width is not given, so a rule applies. The rule is applied using the triangle size given for the whole design at the very beginning of each pattern, and is the basic measurement for all cutting and piecing techniques in that pattern.

Often complete directions will be given for cutting a shape in one value (a light diamond, for example). After that a medium diamond may be required. No additional directions are given, since these are cut exactly the same way as the first diamond. Familiarity will make the methods very easy.

Fabic requirements given for each pattern are for 45" wide pre-washed cotton or cotton blends.

Determining Size of a Finished Quilt

To calculate the size of a finished quilt, two triangle measurements are needed: the perpendicular of the triangle without seam allowance (always ¾" less than **triangle size**), and the length of the triangle **side** without seam allowances, which can be measured with a ruler on the Clearview Triangle. (Or use the table below.)

Multiply the "finished" perpendicular height by the number of triangles in one perpendicular line across the quilt. Multiply the "finished" triangle side by the number of sides across the other quilt dimension.

These two calculations will give you the measurements of the finished size of the quilt.

Table of Finished Triangles
(when using ¼" seams)

Triangle Size	Finished Perpendicular	Finished Side Length
1"	¼"	$5/16$"
2"	1¼"	$1\ 7/16$"
3"	2¼"	$2\ 5/8$"
4"	3¼"	$3\ 13/16$"
5"	4¼"	$4\ 15/16$"
6"	5¼"	$6\ 1/8$"
7"	6¼"	$7\ 1/4$"
8"	7¼"	$8\ 7/16$"
9"	8¼"	$9\ 9/16$"
10"	9¼"	$10\ 3/4$"
11"	10¼"	$11\ 7/8$"
12"	11¼"	$13\ 1/16$"

Note: The diagrams usually consist of combinations of the symbols for individual units (ex. half-diamond ◆) showing proper placement in sections, rows, etc., rather than a sketch of how the seaming actually looks when incomplete. So 2 half-diamonds sewn together would be shown as number 1 rather than number 2 (which is closer to the way they might actually look). Also when individual instructions are not given for a triangle's size, it is the same as the triangle size given at the beginning of the pattern.

Number 1 Number 2

Tumbling Tiles

2″ triangle

Quilt with borders:
32¾″ x 39¼″

Fabric requirements:

⅔ yd. medium fabric
½ yd. light fabric
½ yd. dark fabric

Directions

1. This wall hanging can simply be pieced in vertical rows according to the quilt diagram, or for convenience you may piece 2 units as shown, repeating them in alternating rows. The row that has a light long diamond at the top will repeat unit #1. The row that has a dark long diamond at the top will repeat #2.

2. For each unit cut:
   2 medium 3¼″ triangles
   1 light long diamond from a 1¾″ strip at 3″ on the Clearview Triangle
   1 dark long diamond the reverse of the medium

3. Arrange units (or individual pieces) in vertical rows. Finish the top of each row with a 3¾″ medium triangle half. Finish the bottom of each row with a long diamond matching the one at the top of the row and a 3¾″ medium triangle half. Sew the rows together alternately.

4. Betty added an inner border of ¼″ flat striped piping, a ⅛″ pink border of piping, and a final 3½″ flowered border (mitered).

This little pattern is so open, plain, and simple that it presents an opportunity for special effects. Try a graduated spectrum of your favorite hand-dyed fabrics.

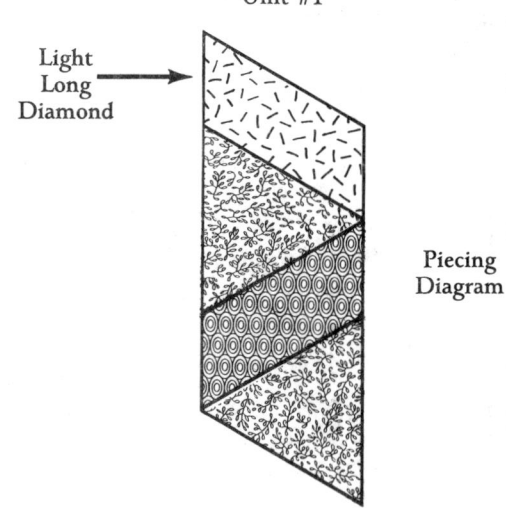

Unit #1 — Light Long Diamond — Piecing Diagram

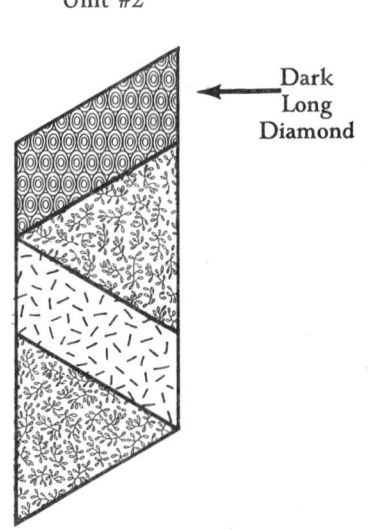

Unit #2 — Dark Long Diamond

Tumbling Tiles

Building Block Quilts 2 – Page twenty-one

Tumbling Bricks

3" triangle

Quilt with borders: 57" x 64½"

Fabric requirements:

¾ yd. light fabric
1 yd. medium fabric
1 yd. dark fabric

Piecing Diagram

Complete Block

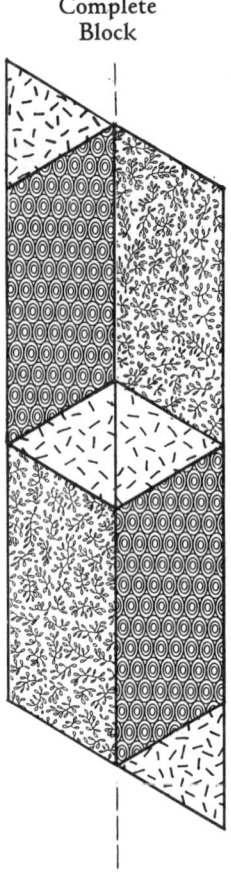

Fill-in Piece

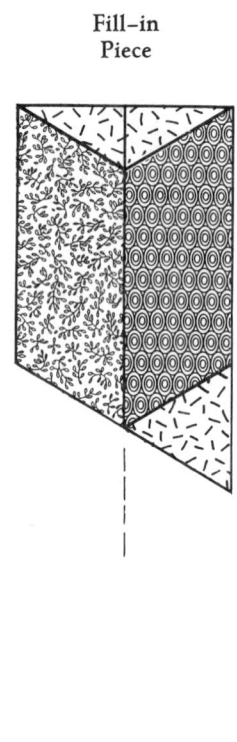

Directions:

1. For each block cut:
   2 dark long diamonds from 2¾" strip at 5" on the Clearview Triangle
   2 medium long diamonds (these are the reverse of the dark long diamonds—see diagram)
   4 light 3" triangles

2. Piece 27 whole blocks and 18 fill-in pieces according to the diagrams above. Use two 3½" light triangle halves, 1 light 3" triangle, and a medium and a dark long diamond in the fill-in piece.

3. Sew 3 blocks into a vertical row. Finish the top and bottom of the row with a fill-in piece. Make 9 rows.

4. Sew the rows together. Add borders as desired. The author used an inner 2" light border, and then an outer 4½" medium border.

Tumbling Bricks

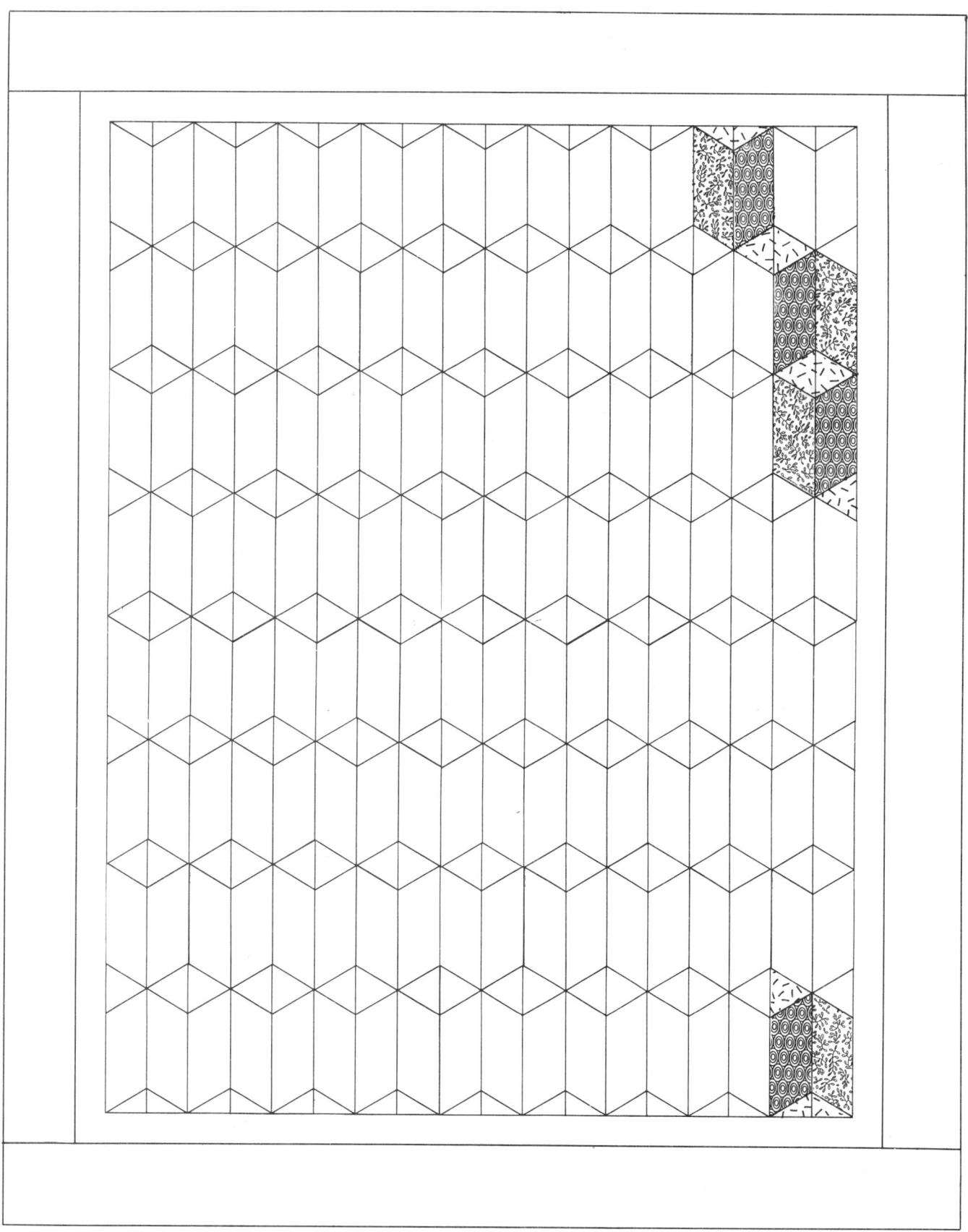

Building Block Quilts 2 – Page twenty-three

Grandmother's Block Garden

3" triangle
Quilt with borders: 72" x 88¾"

Fabric requirements:
1¼ yds. light fabric
1¼ yds. medium fabric
1¼ yds. dark fabric
2½ yds. background fabric

Directions:

1. Cut for each block:
    14 light 3" triangles
    7 medium diamonds
    7 dark diamonds
    4 background triangles
    4 background diamonds

   Assemble in strips according to diagram. Add 7½" background triangles on separate sides of the block as shown. Piece 14 complete blocks.

2. Piece 4 partial blocks. Piece in strips, but at either the top or bottom of each row, add a 2¾" x 4" rectangle, trimmed to a 60° angle as needed. Then sew the rows together.

3. Arrange the Block Gardens in rows as shown in the quilt diagram. The 2 rows that do not end in partial blocks are squared off with background triangle halves cut from a 14¼" x 8¼" rectangle as shown.

4. Sew rows of quilt blocks together. Trim excess off partial blocks at top and bottom. Add a 3" strip of background fabric at left and right side. Lynn added a 2" inner medium green border and a 6¾" outer dark green border.

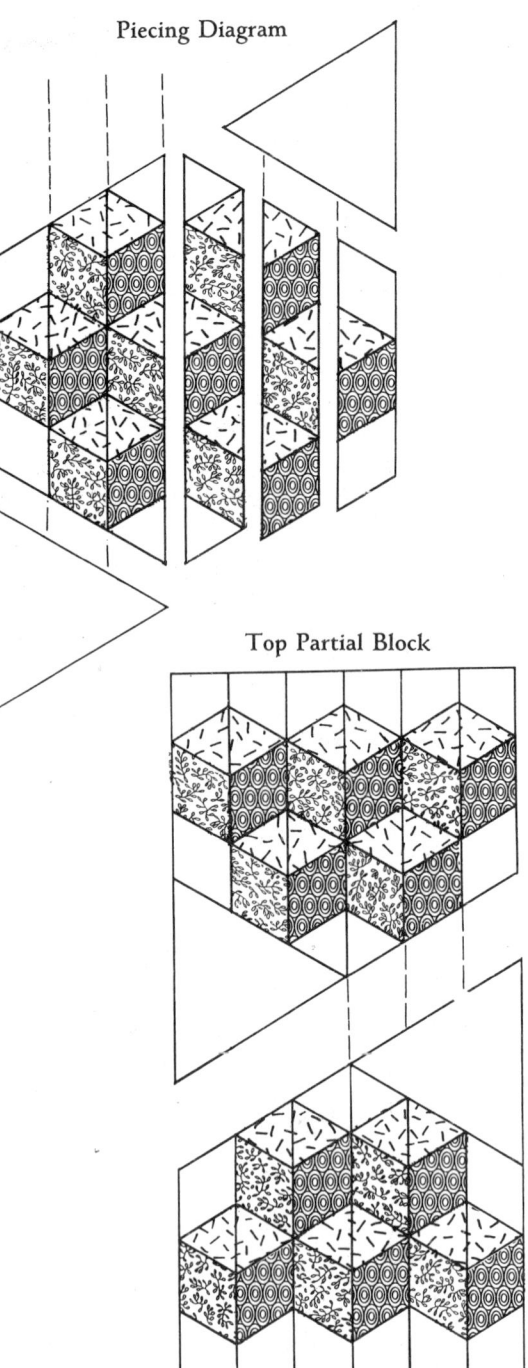

Piecing Diagram

Top Partial Block

Bottom Partial Block

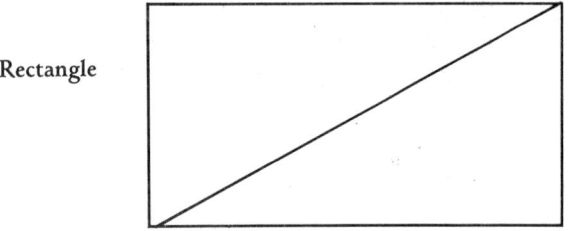

Rectangle

Grandmother's Block Garden

Building Block Quilts 2 — Page twenty-five

Cliff-Dwellers

Page twenty-six — Building Block Quilts 2

Cliff-Dwellers

3″ triangle

Quilt with borders:
56¾″ x 72¾″

Fabric requirements:

1¾ yds. light fabrics
1¾ yds. medium fabrics
2¼ yds. dark fabrics

Directions:

Method #1

(Cut enough pieces for some blocks first, and lay out the pattern to check value choices).

1. Cut:
56 dark flat pyramids from 2¾″ strip at 5¼″ on the Clearview Triangle
35 medium flat pyramids at 5¼″
70 light flat pyramids
45 dark 3″ triangles
45 medium 3″ triangles
86 light 3″ triangles
88 dark diamonds from 2¾″ strip
88 medium diamonds
16 dark triangle halves from 5¾″ triangles
10 background diamond halves from 1⅞″ strip
4 dark triangle halves from 3½″ triangles

2. Assemble flat pyramids and triangles into blocks as shown. Make 40 light-medium (A) and 40 light-dark (B).

3. Make a strip and its reverse from a medium diamond and a dark diamond. Make 40 of each.

4. Assemble blocks and strips into rows A and B. Use 8 light-medium blocks and 8 strips for row A. Use 8 light-dark blocks and 8 reverse strips for row B. End the rows at the top with dark triangle halves from 5¾″ triangles and at the bottom with the correct fill-in pieces as shown in the diagram. Fill-in pieces are made from background diamond halves and either a medium or a dark 3″ triangle.

Block

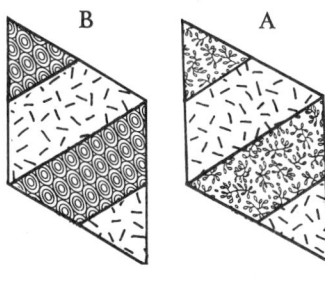

Strip and Reverse

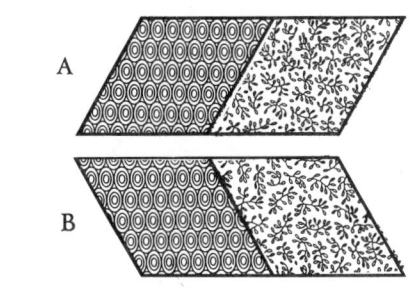

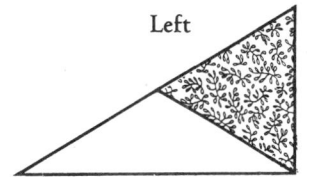 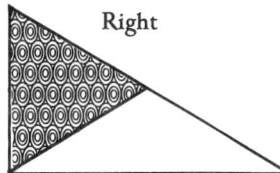

Left   Right

Fill-in Pieces

5. Add a pieced border at the left and right side to complete the pattern as shown in the quilt diagram. The left side border uses background flat pyramids, medium diamonds, light triangles, and 2 background triangle halves from 3½" triangles. The right side border uses dark instead of medium diamonds. Annette added a 3½" border of dark fabric.

Method #2

6. Cut a 2¾" strip each from light and dark fabric. Sew together lengthwise. Press open. From this set of strips (strata) cut triangles at the 5¼" line on the Clearview Triangle. (¼" of the tip will be sticking out above the fabric at the top edge). Sew the 2 different resulting triangles together at the base to produce block B. (40 needed)

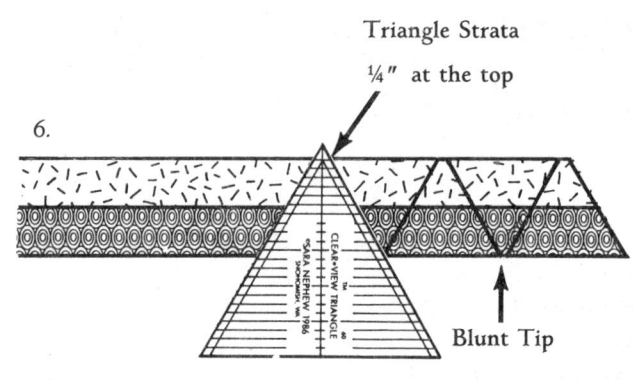

7. Cut a 2¾" strip each from light and medium fabric. Sew into a strata, cut 5¼" triangles, and sew these to produce block A. (40 needed)

8. Cut a 2¾" strip each from dark and medium fabric. Sew into a strata. Cut end of strip at a 60° angle to the right (see diagram). Cut 2¾" sections off the strata to produce strip B. (Check the angle occasionally for accuracy). Cut and sew another dark-medium strata. Cut end of strip at a 60° angle to the left (see diagram). Cut 2¾" sections at this angle to produce strip A. (40 of each strip will be needed).

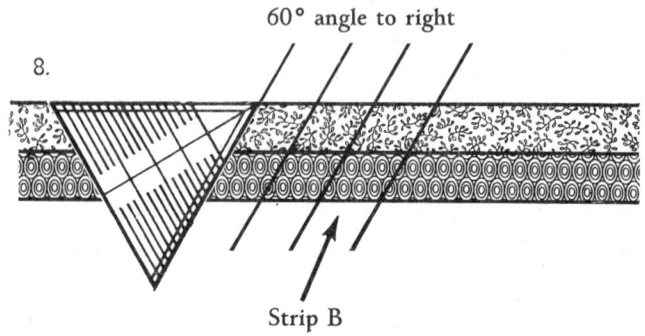

Continue making the quilt as in Direction #4, Method 1.

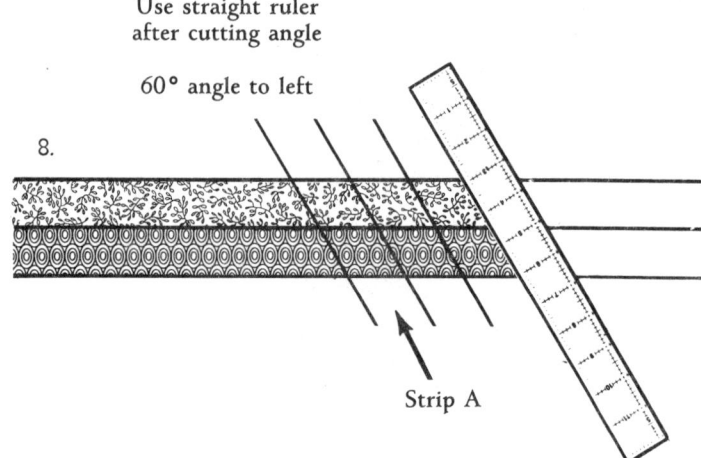

Page twenty-eight — *Building Block Quilts 2*

Tumbling Tiles, 32¾" × 39¼". Flattened blocks in shades of blue and gray show varying lighting effects. More than one value of dark fabric was used, but the light and medium remain the same throughout. Pieced by Betty Parks. (Left)

Stairway, 63½" × 67", is a very graphic quilt. The many shades of black and white call up a feeling of newsprint. Remember the child's riddle "What's black and white and red all over?" Pieced by Charisa Martin. (Right)

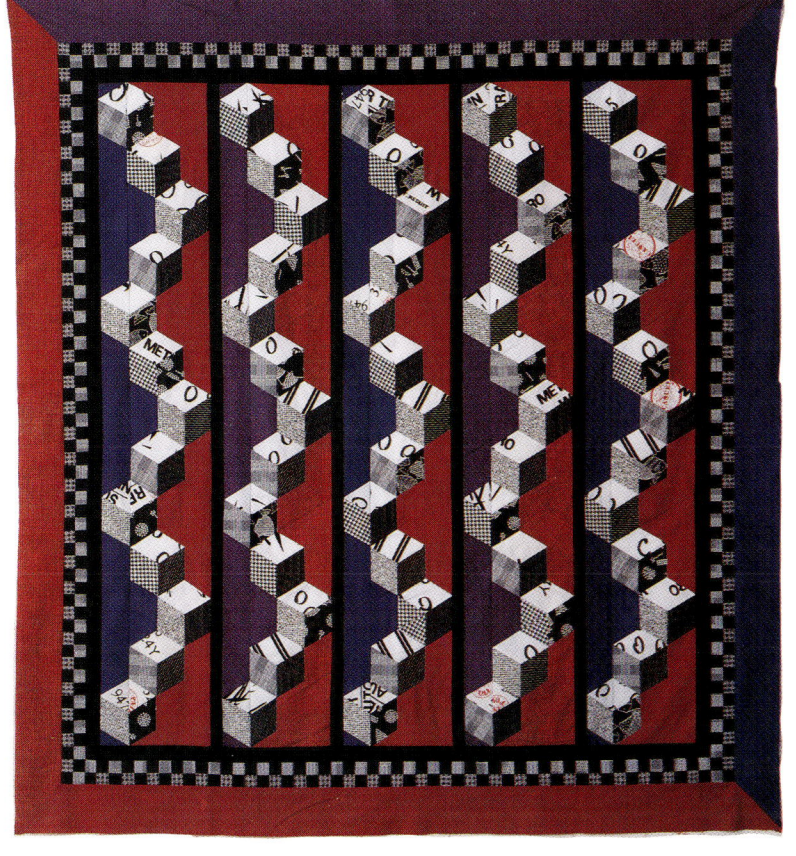

Building Block Quilts 2 — Page twenty-nine

Strippy Quilt, 59" × 79", mixes multi-colored cubes with a busy background to produce a happy, easy to live with quilt. Pieced by Liz Thoman, who calls this quilt "Tropical Fruit, Chunky Style." (Left)

Vistas, 44½" × 52", combines different sizes of the Tumbling Blocks pattern to achieve a greater illusion of depth. The changing scale adds interest to the design. Perhaps the view is reminiscent of a Mediterranean city. Quilted by Beverly Payne. (Right)

Grandmother's Block Garden, 72" × 88¾". The author, like many quilters, has always admired the familiar Grandmother's Flower Garden pattern, but never pieced it. This new pattern has some of the same charm but none of the difficulty. Pieced in flower colors by Lynn Williams and quilted by Pat Beck.

Alphabet Blocks, 52" × 68½", makes a bright child's quilt. Letters and numbers could be added in stencil, applique, or embroidery. Pieced by Mary Pierce. (Top)

Tumbling Bricks, 57" × 64½". This quilt pattern is pieced in elongated blocks that feel elegant to work with. The author had a collection of batik scraps which were added to at the quilt store. Quilted by Beverly Payne. (Bottom Left)

Color Stacks, 45½" × 75", is an example of stripping added to the basic Tumbling Bricks pattern. The carefully graded shading makes the boxes look translucent, lit from within. Like a jewel, this quilt is faceted. Pieced by Laura Munson Reinstatler. (Bottom Right)

Space Crystal, 39½" × 41". Cool colors in the foreground set against warm colors in the background add an electric glow to this multi-dimensional shape. The outer space effect is enhanced by a background fabric of stars. Quilted by the author. (Left)

Endless Chains, 51¼" × 58". Done all in solids, the chains of blocks are so 3-D that it's like a window looking onto a landscape of cubes. Quilted by Pat Beck. (Right)

Building Block Quilts 2 — Page thirty-three

Stream, 54" × 66¾". The curving illusion is produced in this quilt by flattening and lengthening rows of cubes. Streaky and busy fabrics combine with this illusion for a flowing, watery look. The author used both the front and the back of the blue water fabric.

Counterpoint, 42″ × 46½″. This variation of the Wave pattern uses the same fabric in all the sides of a diagonal row of blocks to create crossing curves across the surface of the quilt. Three illusions compete: the curve, the 3-D cubes, and a distance-to-foreground feeling from the top to the bottom. Try turning this page upside down. Quilted by the author. (Top Left)

Frozen Rainbow, 43½″ × 48″. Another version of the Wave pattern combines chintz and grays with solid-colored rows of blocks to emphasize a diagonal curve. The author was reminded of the glacier she had seen in Juneau, Alaska, ice glowing with an inner light. (Top Right)

Diamonds, 81½″ × 103¼″. A pleasing mix of fabrics gives this quilt an old-fashioned look. Colors in the border reflect the color of the nearest block. Pieced by Diane Coombs. (Bottom)

Building Block Quilts 2 — Page thirty-five

Hollow Cube, 32" × 40¾", is pieced in busy florals. When viewed from close up the boxes disappear into swirly patterns, but they reappear quickly when viewed from a distance. Quilted by Beverly Payne. (Top)

Through a Telescope, 68" × 85½". The author began to piece this quilt from 47 different shades and tints of hand-dyed fabric. As work progressed, some greys and beiges were removed, but approximately 36 different colors remain in this quilt. (Bottom Left)

Cliff-Dwellers, 56¾" × 72¾". This is a surprisingly easy quilt. A strip-piecing method makes it fast, or cutting each shape individually would provide greater opportunities for special shading effects. A bold Christmas quilt in these colors, it brings to mind piles of gift boxes. Pieced by Annette Austin and quilted by Beverly Payne. (Bottom Right)

Strippy Quilt (With Fleur-de-Lis)

3" triangle

Quilt with border: 59" x 79"

Fabric requirements:

½ yd. light fabric
½ yd. medium fabric
½ yd. dark fabric
1¼ yds. background fabric
1½ yds. for strips and borders

Directions:

1. Cut for each Fleur-de-Lis block:
   - 8 light 3" triangles
   - 4 medium diamonds from 2¾" strip
   - 4 dark diamonds
   - 4 background diamonds
   - 2 background 5¼" triangles

   Assemble each block in rows according to the diagram. Add a 5¼" background triangle on separate ends as shown.

2. Make 12 Fleur-de-Lis Blocks. Sew into 3 rows of blocks. Piece 3 blocks to finish the row with 5¾" background triangle halves at the top or bottom as shown.

3. Piece 3 partial blocks. For the 2 top partial blocks, cut:
   - 2 light triangles
   - 3 medium diamonds
   - 3 dark diamonds
   - 2 background diamonds
   - 4 light 3½" triangle halves

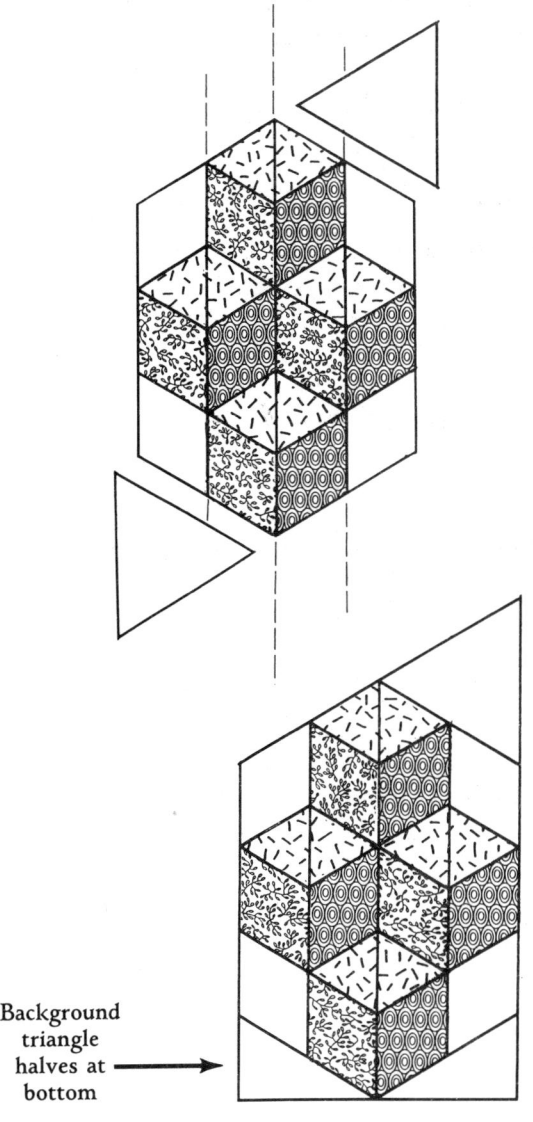

Piecing Diagram

Background triangle halves at bottom →

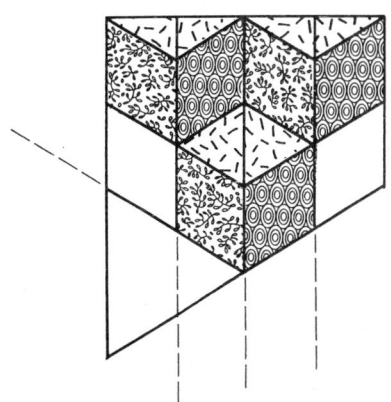

Top Partial Block

For a bottom partial block cut:
6 light triangles
1 medium diamond
1 dark diamond
2 medium rectangles 2¾" x 4"
2 dark rectangles 2¾" x 4"

(Trim the rectangles to a 60° angle according to the diagram). Sew the partial blocks each according to the diagram. Sew to the top or the bottom of a row of blocks. Trim the rectangles as necessary after quilt top is complete.

4. Construct Block Borders. Border #2 is pieced in Block units as shown. Finish top and bottom with 3½" background triangle halves. **Border #2 is used as the measure for all the other pieced rows and setting strips.** Border #1 is pieced in 3 rows using light triangles, medium and dark diamonds, and background flat pyramids cut at 5¼" on the Clearview Triangle. Finish top and bottom 3 rows with 2¾" x 4" background rectangles trimmed to a 60° angle.

5. Measure Block Border #2. Trim other pieced rows to the same length, trimming off the excess in the rectangles. Cut 2¾" strips of the background fabric(s) the same length as the pieced rows. Use these as setting strips between all the rows. Liz used the same fabric for a 2½" border around the outside. To make a larger quilt, make more blocks and more rows.

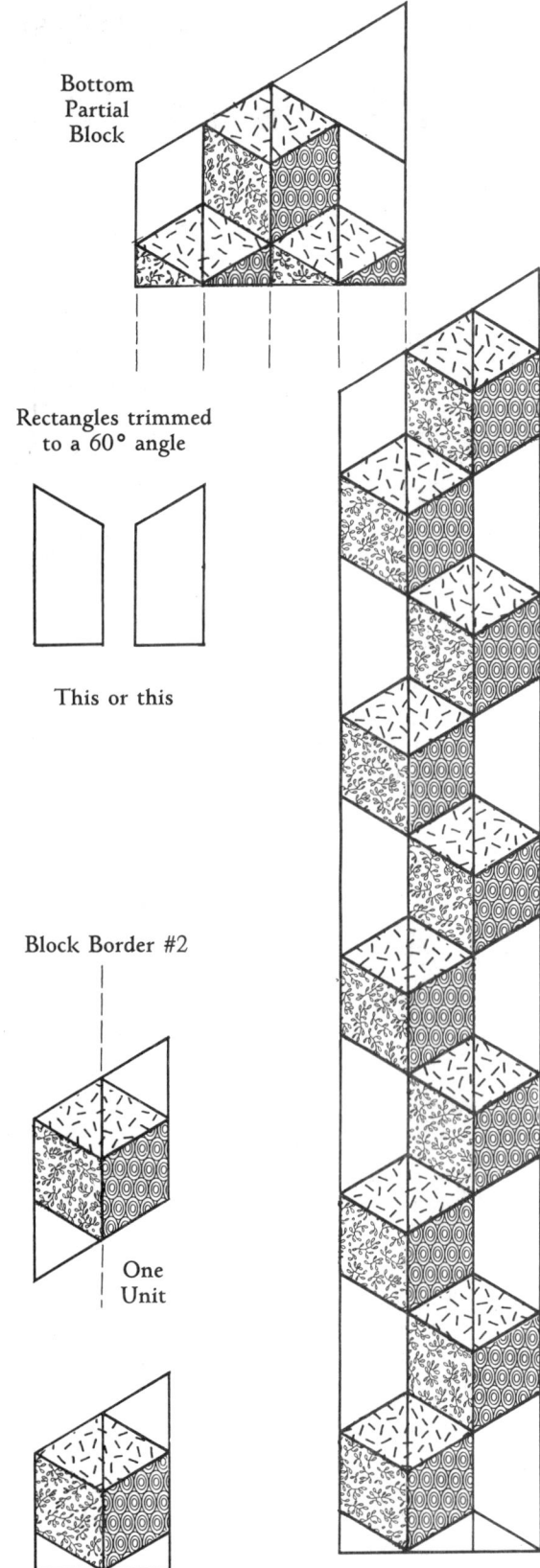

Page thirty-eight — *Building Block Quilts 2*

Strippy Quilt (With Fleur-de-Lis)

Alphabet Blocks

3" triangle

Quilt with borders: 52" x 68½"

Fabric requirements:

½ yd. light fabric
½ yd. medium fabric
½ yd. dark fabric
2⅓ yds. background fabric

Directions:

1. Cut for each block:
    - 12 light 3" triangles
    - 6 dark diamonds
    - 6 medium diamonds
    - 2 background 3" triangles
    - 4 background diamonds
    - 2 background diamonds at 5" on the Clearview Triangle

  Assemble in rows according to the diagram.

2. Complete each block with a 7½" background triangle at opposite sides as shown. Make 6 blocks.

3. Sew blocks into 2 rows as shown in the quilt diagram. Finish top and bottom of each row with 10" background triangle halves cut from a 10" x 5¾" rectangle as shown.

4. Add a 4" setting strip of background fabric in the center and a 2¾" strip at left and right edge of the quilt top. Trim quilt to 1½" from top and bottom of blocks.

5. Make Marching Blocks border. Side, top, and bottom units are separated by 1½" strips of background fabric. After top and bottom borders are pieced, measure them and if necessary trim quilt width slightly to match. Piece side borders. Cut a strip of background fabric the same width as the side borders (5¼"). Cut strip to 4 equal lengths. Trim each to a 60° angle and use to finish top and bottom of side border. Sew to quilt, matching centers. Mary added a 3½" final border of the background fabric.

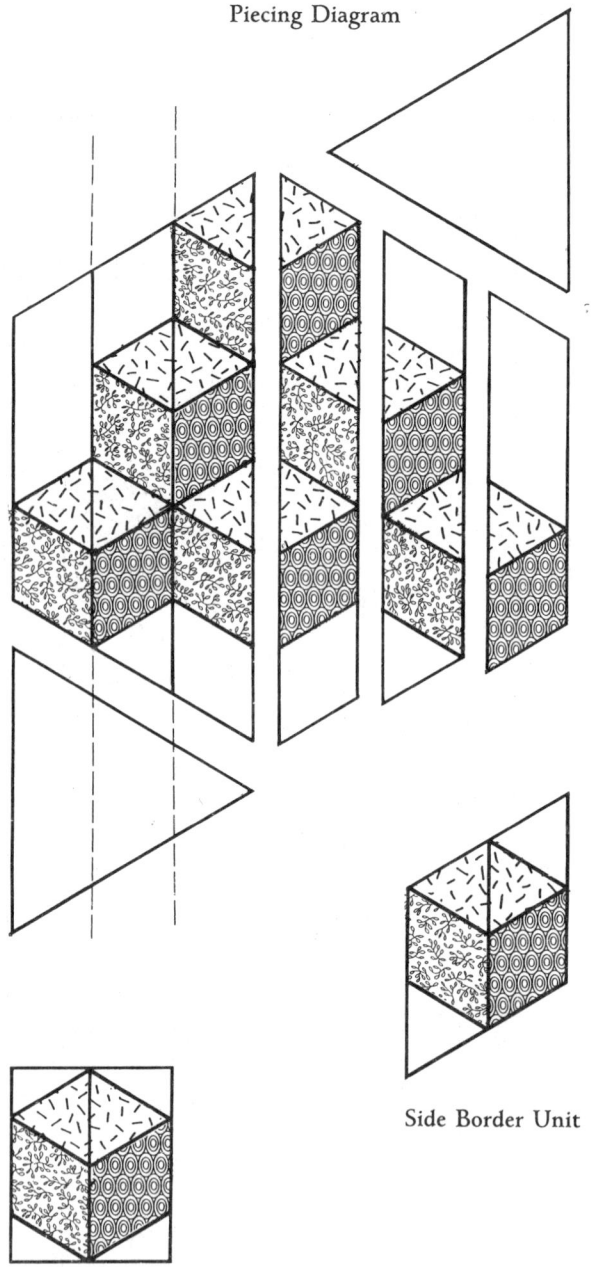

Piecing Diagram

Side Border Unit

Top and Bottom Border Unit

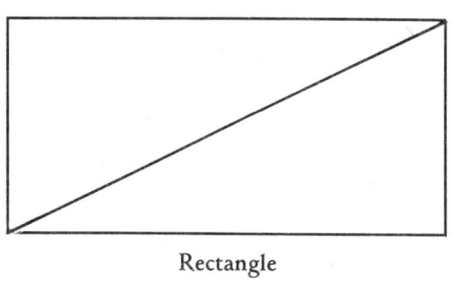

Rectangle

Alphabet Blocks

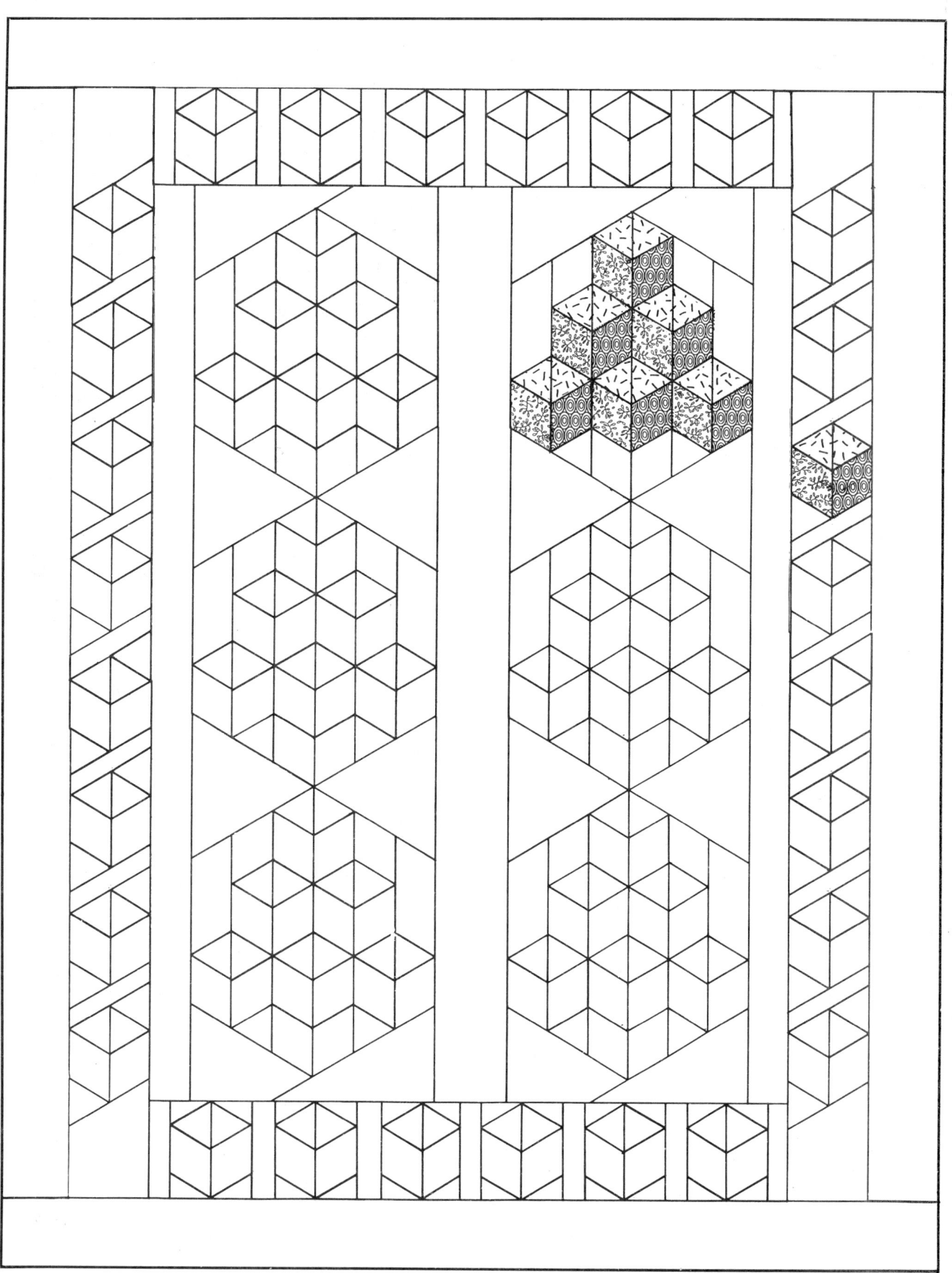

Building Block Quilts 2 — Page forty-one

Diamonds

3" triangle

Quilt with borders: 81½" x 103¼"

Fabric requirements:

1¼ yds. light fabric
1¼ yds. medium fabric
1¼ yds. dark fabric
1¾ yds. background fabric

Directions:

1. Cut for each block:
    18 light 3" triangles
    9 medium diamonds from 2¾" strip
    9 dark diamonds
    4 background diamonds
    4 background long diamonds cut at 5"
       on the Clearview Triangle
   Assemble in rows according to the diagram.
   DO NOT SEW THE CENTER SEAM.

2. Piece 25 blocks. Do not sew the center seam. Arrange and sew half-blocks in 10 rows according to the quilt diagram. Finish top and bottom of each row with an 8" background triangle half. Sew the rows together. Diane added a 4¼" border of background fabric, a multi-colored border of flat pyramids and a final 1¼" strip of black.

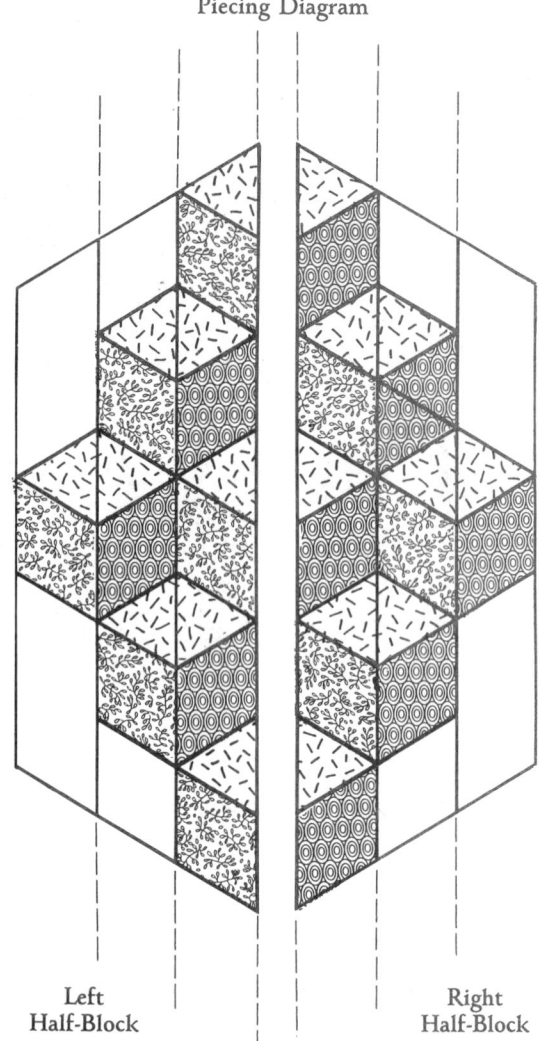

Piecing Diagram

Left Half-Block

Right Half-Block

Diamonds

Building Block Quilts 2 – Page forty-three

Hollow Cube

4½″ triangle

Quilt with border: 32″ x 40¾″

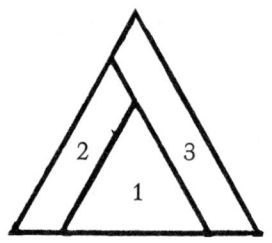
Piecing Diagram

Fabric requirements:

½ yd. light fabric
½ yd. medium fabric
½ yd. dark fabric
1 yd. border fabric

Directions:

1. Cut for 1 block:
   2 each dark, medium, and light 3″ triangles
   2 each flat pyramids from dark, medium, and light fabric cut from 1¼″ strip at 3¾″ on the Clearview Triangle
   2 each flat pyramids from dark, medium, and light fabric cut from 1¼″ strip at 4½″ on the Clearview Triangle

Suggestion: Cut enough pieces at a time for only a few blocks, to better control and adjust value choices.

2. Make 6 log-cabin pieced triangles according to the diagram. Sew 3¾″ flat pyramid to one side of the triangle and press out. Sew 4½″ flat pyramid to the other side. Choose values for the triangle and the flat pyramids carefully, following the diagram.

3. Sew into half-blocks as shown. (**Do not sew the center seam**). Sew alternate left and right half-blocks into vertical rows as in the quilt diagram. Finish the top of each row with a 5″ dark triangle half, and the bottom of each row with a 5″ light triangle half. Sew the rows together. The author added a 5¾″ dark floral border.

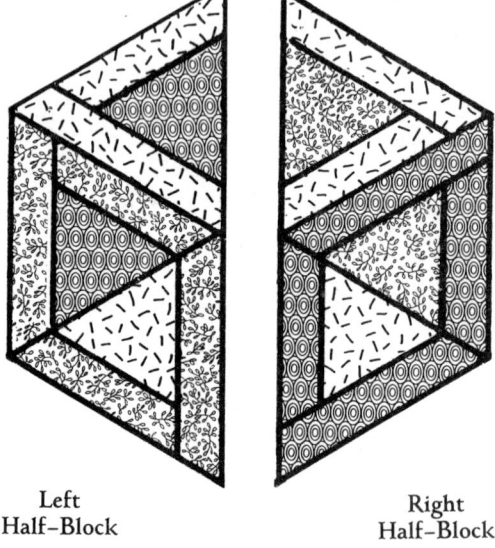

Left Half-Block   Right Half-Block

Another Method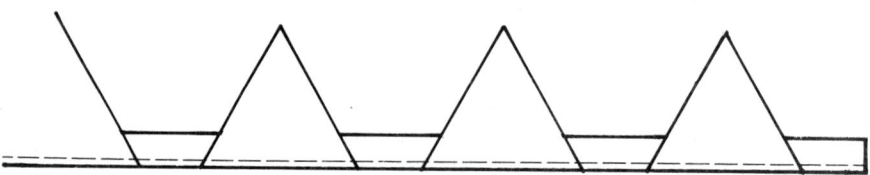

If sewing triangles to a long strip, leave at least 2X strip width between them.

Hollow Cube

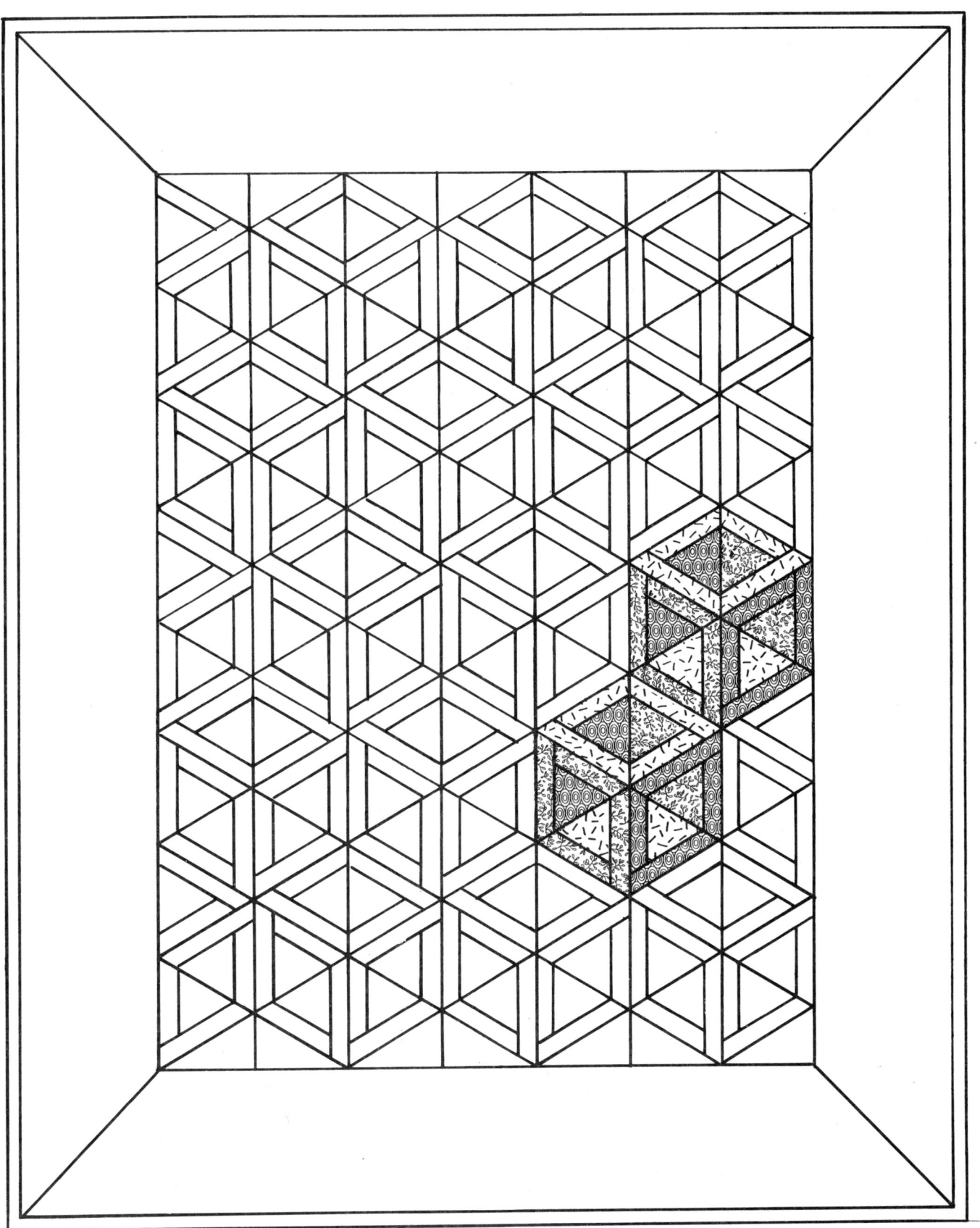

Building Block Quilts 2 — Page forty-five

Stairway

3" triangle

Quilt with borders: 63½" x 67"

Fabric requirements:

¾ yd. light fabric
¾ yd. medium fabric
¾ yd. dark fabric
¾ yd. dark background fabric
¾ yd. medium background fabric
additional fabric for borders

Directions:

1. Cut for each block #1:
    - 1 medium diamond
    - 2 light diamonds
    - 2 dark triangles
    - 1 medium triangle
    - 1 dark background flat pyramid cut at 5¼" on the Clearview Triangle
    - 1 medium background diamond
    - 1 medium background 5¼" triangle

    Cut for each block #2:
    - 2 dark diamonds from a 2¾" strip
    - 1 medium diamond
    - 1 light diamond
    - 2 dark triangles
    - 1 medium triangle
    - 1 light triangle
    - 2 medium background flat pyramids cut at 5¼" on the Clearview Triangle

3. Piece 15 of block #1 and 15 of block #2. Assemble in 5 rows according to the quilt diagram (alternating blocks #1 and #2). Finish bottom of row with 7¾" medium background triangle half cut from 7¾" x 4½" rectangle as shown. Finish top of row with fill-in piece made from: 1 dark diamond, 1 light triangle, 1 medium background triangle, and 1 medium background half-diamond cut from 3" strip.

4. Add a strip to the left side of each row of blocks to complete the design. Each strip is pieced from:
    - 4 light triangles
    - 4 medium diamonds
    - 3 dark background flat pyramids cut from a 2¾" strip at 12" on the Clearview Triangle
    - 2 dark background 3½" triangle halves

5. Sew the 5 completed rows together. Charisa separated each row with a 1½" strip of black. Then she added a 1¾" black inner border, a border of 1½" squares, and a final 4" red border.

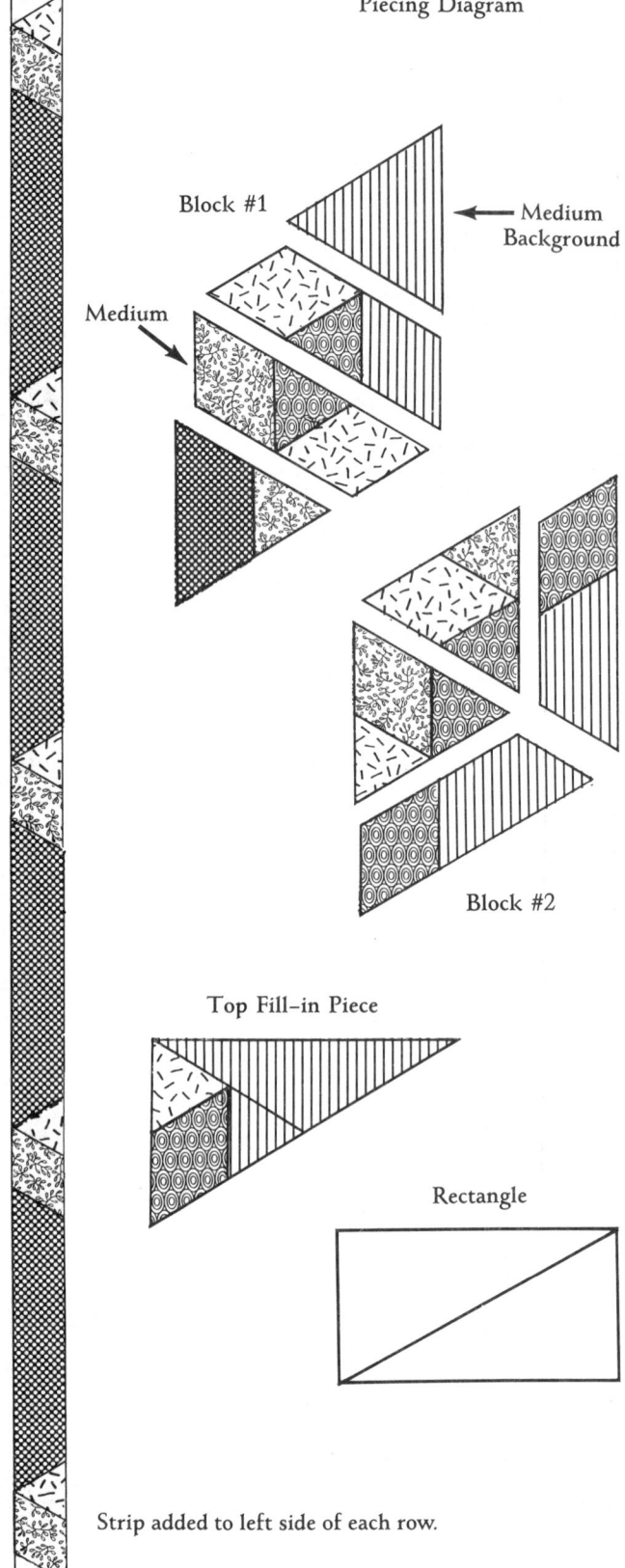

Piecing Diagram

Block #1 — Medium Background

Medium

Block #2

Top Fill-in Piece

Rectangle

Strip added to left side of each row.

Stairway

Endless Chains

3" triangle

Quilt with borders: 51¼" x 58"

Fabric requirements:

1 yd. light fabric
1 yd. medium fabric
1 yd. dark fabric
1¼ yds. background fabric
1¾ yds. border fabric

Note: With a little planning, chains of color can run diagonally across this quilt. Find all your solid scraps and make an "Amish" quilt. You will need a wall, table, or some floor space on which to arrange the blocks. Color diagonal rows on the quilt diagram. Then count how many of each color are needed in Block #1 and Block #2. Block #1 is always all one color. The color change occurs in Block #2.

Directions:

1. For each block #1 cut:
   1 dark diamond from 2¾" strip
   1 medium diamond
   1 dark triangle
   1 medium triangle
   2 light triangles

2. For each block #2 cut:
   2 background diamonds
   1 light diamond
   1 medium triangle
   1 dark triangle

3. Piece 34 each of block #1 and block #2. In addition, piece 2 each of 2 top half-blocks and 2 bottom half-blocks.

4. Sew blocks alternately into rows, following the quilt diagram. Odd-numbered rows begin and end with a complete block, either #1 or #2. Even-numbered rows begin and end with the required half-block.

5. Complete the top and bottom of each row with a fill-in piece. In rows 2, 6, 3, and 7 make the fill-in piece using a 2¾" x 3½" piece of the required fabric (see diagrams). Trim even with the edge of the top after the rows are sewn together.

Top and Bottom Fill-in Piece

Rows 1, 5, 9   Rows 2, 6   Rows 3, 7   Rows 4, 8

The author added a 9" medium gray border and a 2½" black border to bring out the Amish look.

Piecing Diagram

Block #1   Block #2

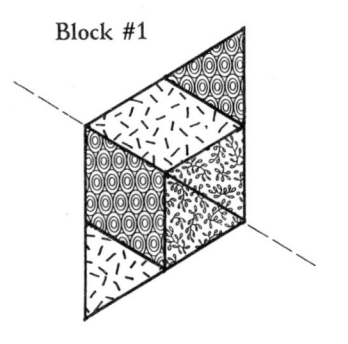 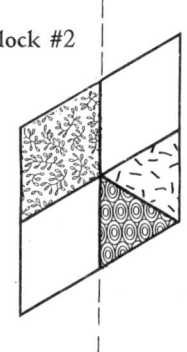

Half-Blocks

3.   Top

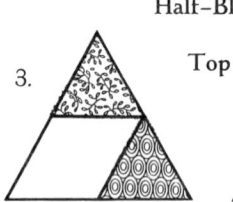 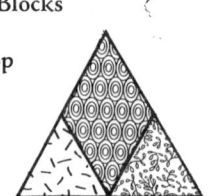

Bottom

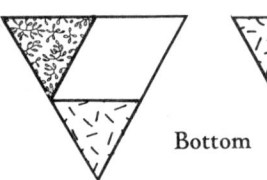

Top and Bottom Fill-in Piece

Rows 1, 5, 9   Rows 2, 6

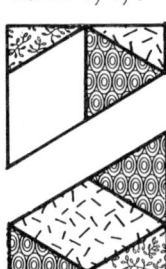 

Rows 3, 7   Rows 4, 8

Endless Chains

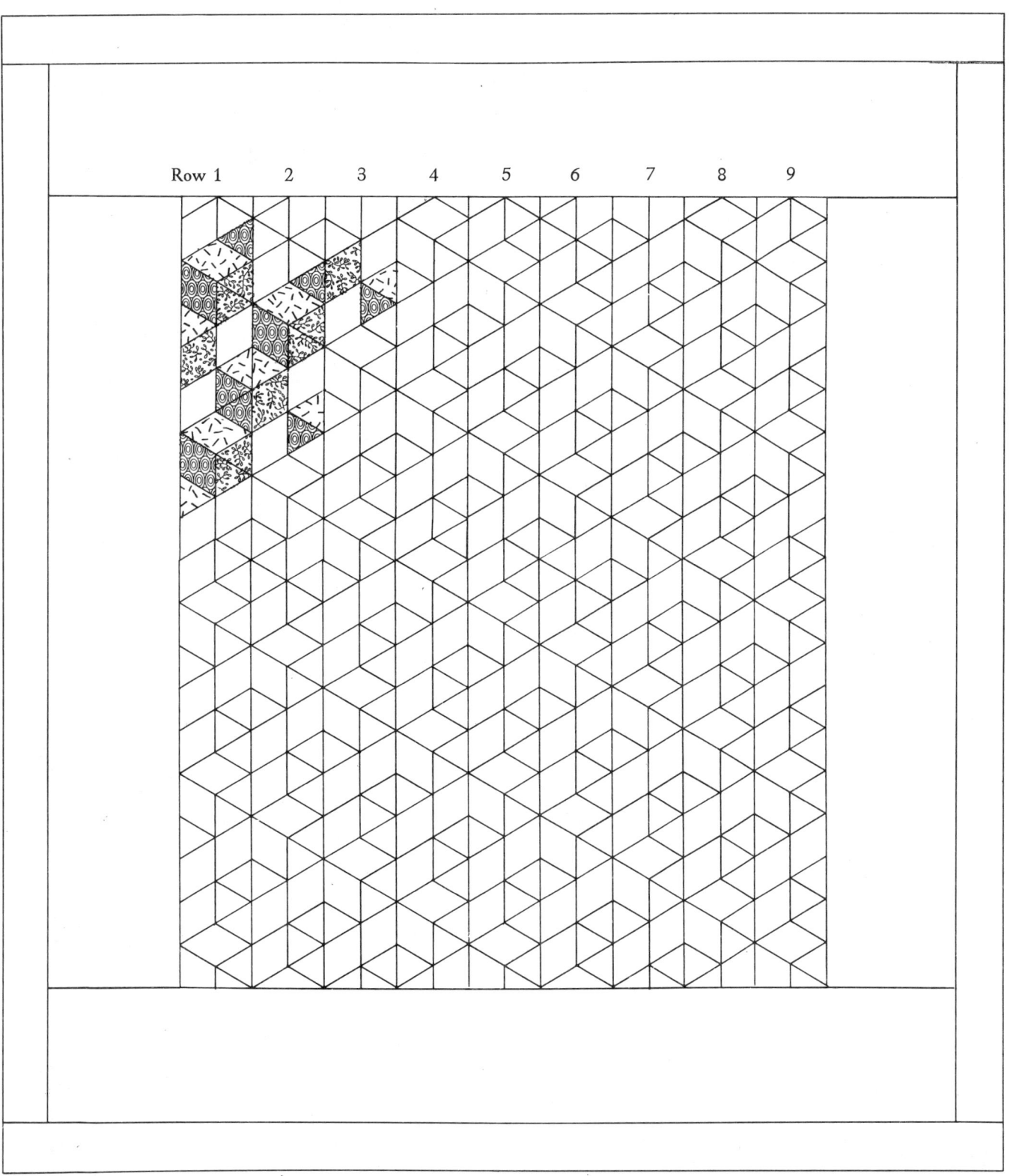

Building Block Quilts 2 — Page forty-nine

Vistas

Quilt with borders: 44½" x 52"

Triangle Sizes: 3¾" (large center panel)
  3" (medium sized panels)
  2¼" (small outside panels)

Fabric requirements:

Large panel—½ yd. each
  dark, medium and light fabric
Middle-sized panel—½ yd. each
  dark, medium and light fabric
Small panel—⅓ yd. each
  dark, medium and light fabric

Directions:

1. Cut for each block according to the rules given in the cutting directions:
   1 dark triangle (from a strip the width of triangle size)
   1 medium triangle
   1 light triangle
   1 dark diamond (¼" narrower than triangle size)
   1 medium diamond
   1 light diamond

2. Assemble as shown. Make complete blocks from 2 half-blocks.

3. Piece 3 large blocks, 10 middle-sized blocks, and 21 small blocks.

4. Using a half-block, a dark triangle, a medium diamond, a light triangle half left side, (the right side will be used in #5), and a light diamond half (see table below), assemble a partial block. You will need 1 partial block each for the large size, 2 for the middle size and 3 for the small.

5. Using a dark diamond, a medium triangle, a light triangle half (right side) and a light diamond half, assemble a fill-in piece. You will need the same number as the partial blocks above.

6. Make 1 row of large blocks, 2 rows of middle-sized blocks, and 3 rows of small blocks. Trim the middle sized rows as necessary to achieve equal length with the others. Sew the rows together according to the diagram. Add a 1½" strip between the inner rows and a darker 1" strip between the outer rows.

7. Add outer left and right borders to complete the blocks at the left and right (based on 2¼" triangle-flat pyramid is cut at 3¾"). Finish with a 5" border.

Piecing Diagram

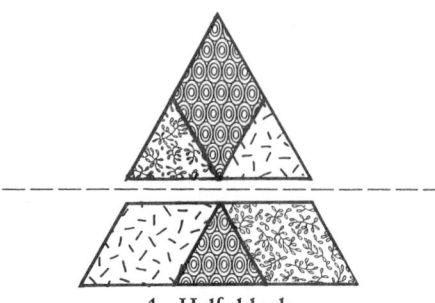

1. Half-block

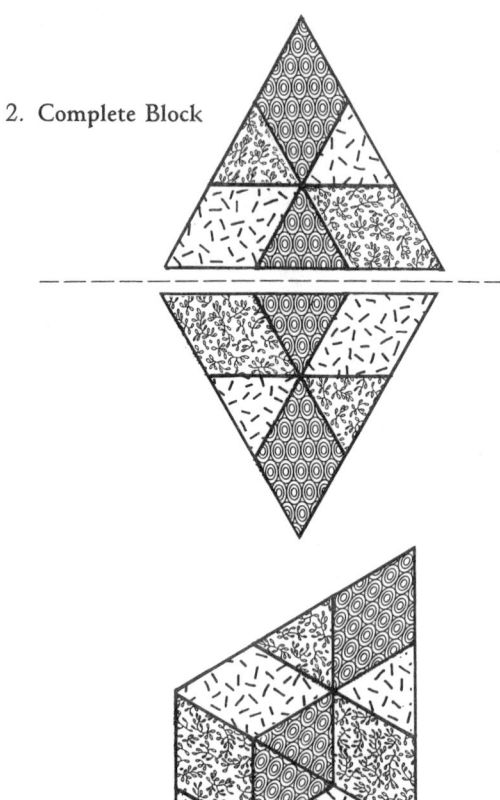

2. Complete Block

4. Partial Block

5. Fill-in Piece

Half-Diamond Table

triangle size	strip width
3¾"	2⅜"
3	1⅞"
2¼"	1⅜"

Vistas

Building Block Quilts 2 — Page fifty-one

Through a Telescope

Through a Telescope

Triangle size: 3¾", 3", 2¼"

Quilt with borders: 68" x 85½"

Fabric requirements:

Light group — ½ yd. each light, medium, and dark fabrics
Medium group — ½ yd. each light, medium, and dark fabrics
Dark group — ¾ yd. each light, medium, and dark fabrics

¼ yd. background fabric
Choose the background fabric after piecing all the other sections of the quilt.

Directions:

If working with many colors, better results may be achieved by laying out the blocks as they are pieced.

Important! Sew the center seam last!
(See instruction #6)

1. From the **light group** of fabrics make 7 top half-blocks and 7 bottom half-blocks based on 3¾" triangle size (3¾" triangle, diamond from 3½" strip, flat pyramid from 3½" strip at 6¾" on the Clearview Triangle). Arrange and sew into 2 rows according to the quilt diagram for the center section. Complete the bottom of each row with a left or right fill-in piece as shown (flat pyramid, triangle, diamond, and long diamond cut from 3½" strip at 6½" on Clearview Triangle). *Do not sew the left and right rows together.*

2. From the medium group of fabrics make 11 top half-blocks and 11 bottom half-blocks based on 3" triangle size. Arrange into 4 rows according to the quilt diagram, left and right of center. Complete the bottom of each row with a left or right fill-in piece. Sew rows into left and right sections. (Pieces are cut according to the rules or according to the *Table of Common Shapes*).

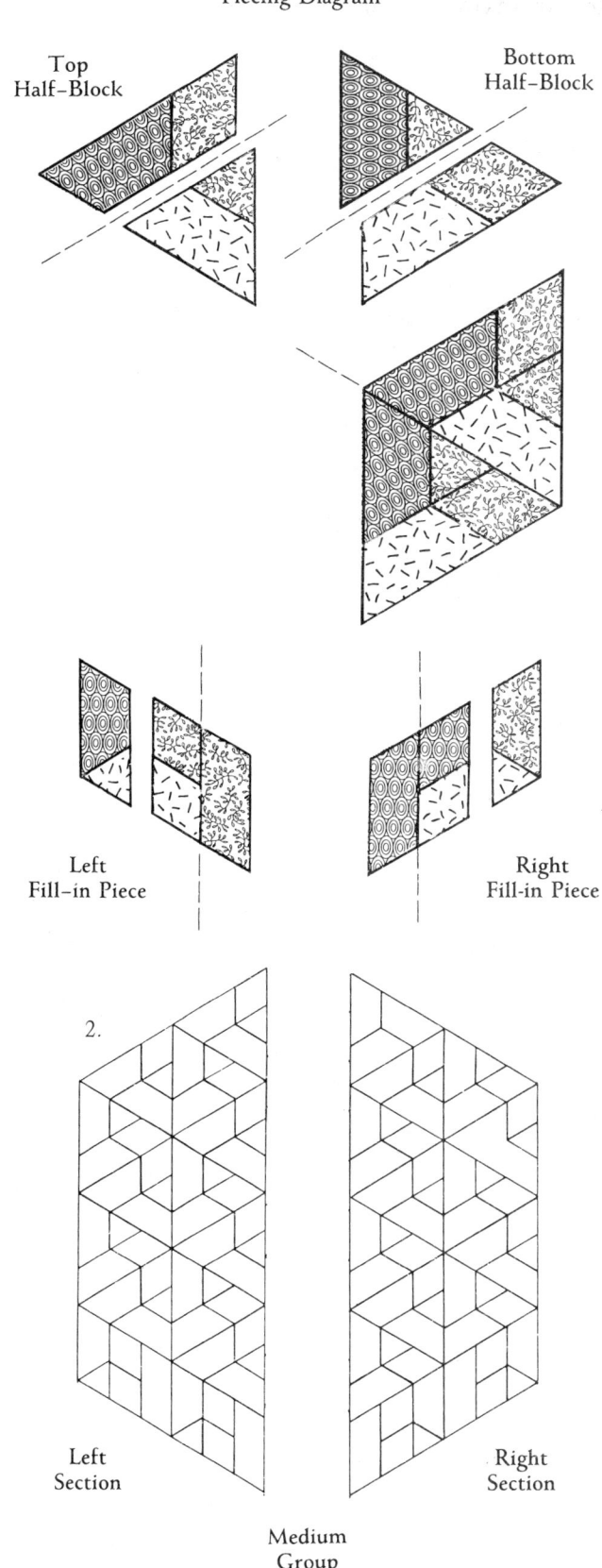

Piecing Diagram

Top Half-Block | Bottom Half-Block

Left Fill-in Piece | Right Fill-in Piece

2.

Left Section | Right Section

Medium Group

3. From the darkest group of fabrics make 16 top half-blocks and 16 bottom half-blocks based on 2¼" triangle size. Arrange the top left and right rows according to the quilt diagram. Complete the tops of the rows with top edge pieces as shown. Complete the bottoms of the rows with (A) bottom fill-in pieces. Sew rows into left and right sections.

4. Take the half-blocks left from #3 above and arrange in rows at the bottom of the quilt according to the diagram. Complete the bottoms of the rows with bottom edge pieces. Complete the tops of the rows with (B) top fill-in pieces. Sew rows into left and right sections.

5. When all eight sections are complete choose and insert the background fabric(s). Sew a 1¼" strip of background fabric to the top and bottom of each center row. Sew a 2" strip of background fabric to the top and bottom of each left and right side section. Sew left and right sections to left and right center rows, centering with pins. *Do not sew center seam.*

6. Sew the dark top and bottom sections to the center sections. Sew center seam from top to bottom. The author added a 4" medium brown inner border, a 2" pink border, and a 3½" maroon outside border.

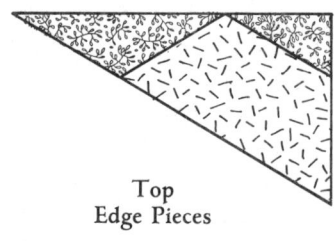

Top Edge Pieces

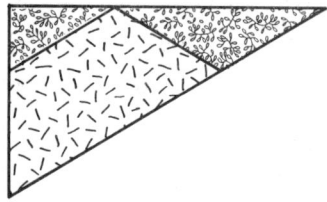

Bottom Edge Pieces

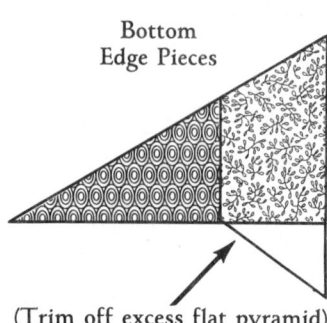

(Trim off excess flat pyramid)

(Flat pyramid and 4¼" triangle half)

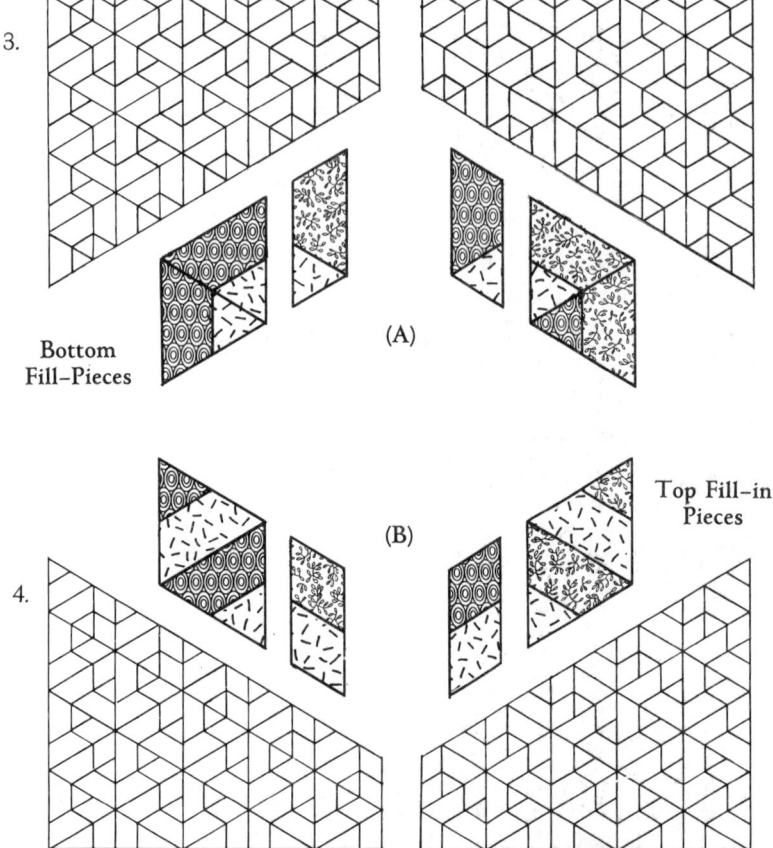

3.

Bottom Fill-Pieces

(A)

(B)

Top Fill-in Pieces

4.

Page fifty-four — *Building Block Quilts 2*

Wave

3" triangle   (4" triangle)

Quilt without borders:
27" x 31½"   (39½" x 46¼")

Fabric requirements:

1 yd. (1½ yds.) light fabric
1 yd. (1½ yds.) medium fabric
1 yd. (1½ yds.) dark fabric

Plus additional border fabric.

Note: Follow the block piecing directions given below, or piece in 2 vertical rows, repeating these.

PRESSING HINT: Press toward the triangle.

Directions:

1. For Block #1 cut:
    4 light 3" (4") triangles
    2 medium long diamonds cut from 2¾" (3¾")
      strip at 1⅝" (2¼") width (see diagrams below)
    2 dark long diamonds cut from 2¾" (3¾")
      strip at 1⅝" (2¼") width
   Assemble according to the diagram.
   Make 5 more of these.

2. For Block #2 cut:
    4 light 3" (4") triangles
    2 medium diamonds
    2 dark diamonds
   Assemble according to the diagram.
   Make 5 more of these.

Piecing Diagram

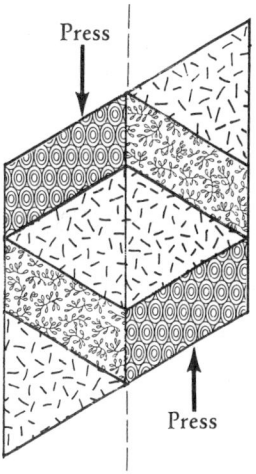

Block #1

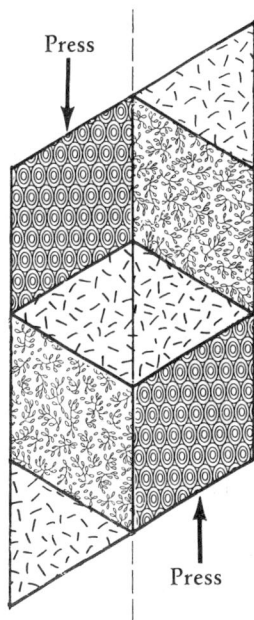

Block #2

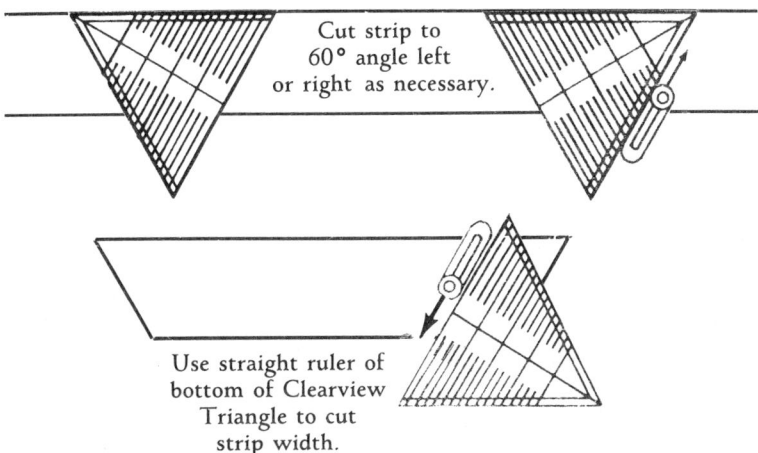

Cut strip to 60° angle left or right as necessary.

Use straight ruler of bottom of Clearview Triangle to cut strip width.

Building Block Quilts 2 — Page fifty-five

Wave

3. For Block #3 cut:
    4 light 3″ (4″) triangles
    1 medium diamond
    1 dark diamond
    1 medium long diamond cut from 2¾″ (3¾″) strip at 3⅞″ (5⅜″) on the Clearview Triangle
    1 dark reverse long diamond cut from 2¾″ (3¾″) strip at 3⅞″ (5⅜″)

Assemble according to the diagram.
Make 5 more of these.

Block #3

4. For Top Finishing Piece cut:
    1 light 3″ triangle
    1 medium long diamond cut from 2¾″ (3¾″) strip at 1⅝″ (2¼″) width
    1 dark reverse long diamond cut from 2¾″ (3¾″) strip at 1⅝″ (2¼″) width
    2 light triangle halves from a 3½″ (4½″) triangle

Assemble according to the diagram.
Make 5 more of these.

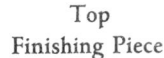

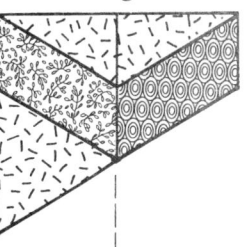

Top Finishing Piece

5. For Bottom Finishing Piece cut:
    1 light 3″ (4″) triangle
    1 medium long diamond cut from 2¾″ (3¾″) strip at 5″ (7″) on the Clearview Triangle
    1 dark reverse long diamond cut from 2¾″ (3¾″) strip at 5″ (7″)
    2 light triangle halves from a 3½″ (4½″) triangle

Assemble according to the diagram.
Make 5 more of these.

Bottom Finishing Piece

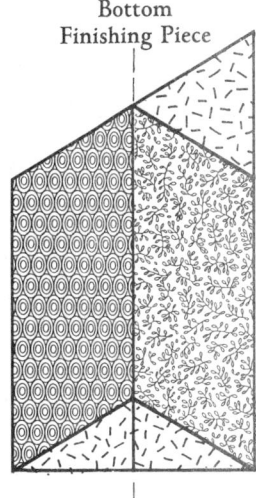

6. Assemble each vertical row according to the quilt diagram from blocks #1, #2, #3, and Top and Bottom finishing pieces. Sew 6 vertical rows together for the quilt top. (Or assemble from the quilt diagram vertical rows 1 and 2 without using block instructions. Repeat these each 6 times). The author added a 2¾″ medium inner border and a 5½″ dark outer border to **"Counterpoint"** and a 6½″ light inner border and 2½″ outer medium border to **"Glacier."**

Stream

3" triangle

Quilt with borders: 54" x 66¾"

Fabric requirements:

1¾ yds. light fabric(s)
1¾ yds. medium fabric(s)
1¾ yds. dark fabric(s)
additional darks plus ⅓ yd. black for border

The author chose to make separate diagonal streams, each gently curving diagonal stream a light, medium, and dark fabric of one color—with some breaks and direction changes. Copies of the quilt diagram were colored first, until a pleasing arrangement was found. Then fabrics were chosen to follow the diagram as the blocks were assembled, concentrating on one vertical row at a time.

Directions:

1. Assemble blocks #1, #2, and #3 as in the *Wave* quilt on pg. 55. No Top Finishing Pieces are needed, as the Bottom Finishing Piece is used at the top also.

2. Make 20 of Block #1, 20 of Block #2, 20 of Block #3, and 20 of the Bottom Finishing Piece. Assemble into 20 vertical rows according to the quilt diagram. (At the top, Block #3 is upside down.) Sew the rows together.

3. For the border, choose dark fabrics used in the quilt. Cut 1", 2", and 3" strips. Sew together at random into 2 sets of strips, adding or subtracting colors as desired. Cut the end of each set of strips to a 60° angle. Cut 5" sections from this end, checking the 60° angle often. Sew the 5" widths together, inserting a black strip occasionally. Continue border ends with 5" black section at each corner. (Cut to a 60° angle and sew to stripped border.) Border ends sew across other border counterclockwise. Start by not sewing first border all the way to left corner. Leave a few inches unsewn. Sew on each border to the right. Then sew the remaining portion of the first border.

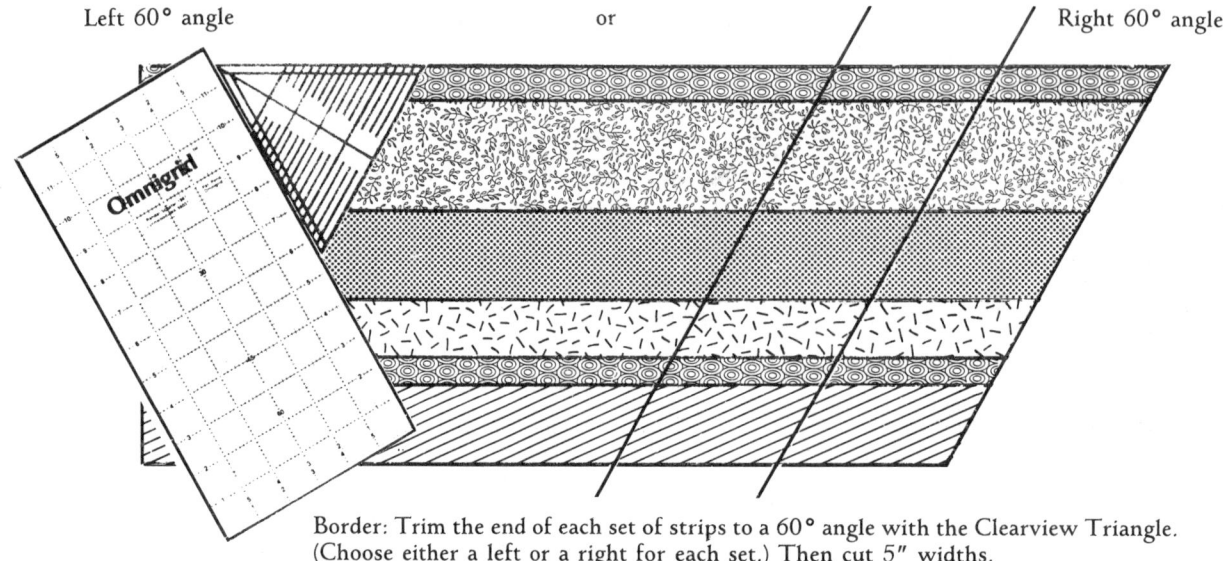

Border: Trim the end of each set of strips to a 60° angle with the Clearview Triangle. (Choose either a left or a right for each set.) Then cut 5" widths.

Stream

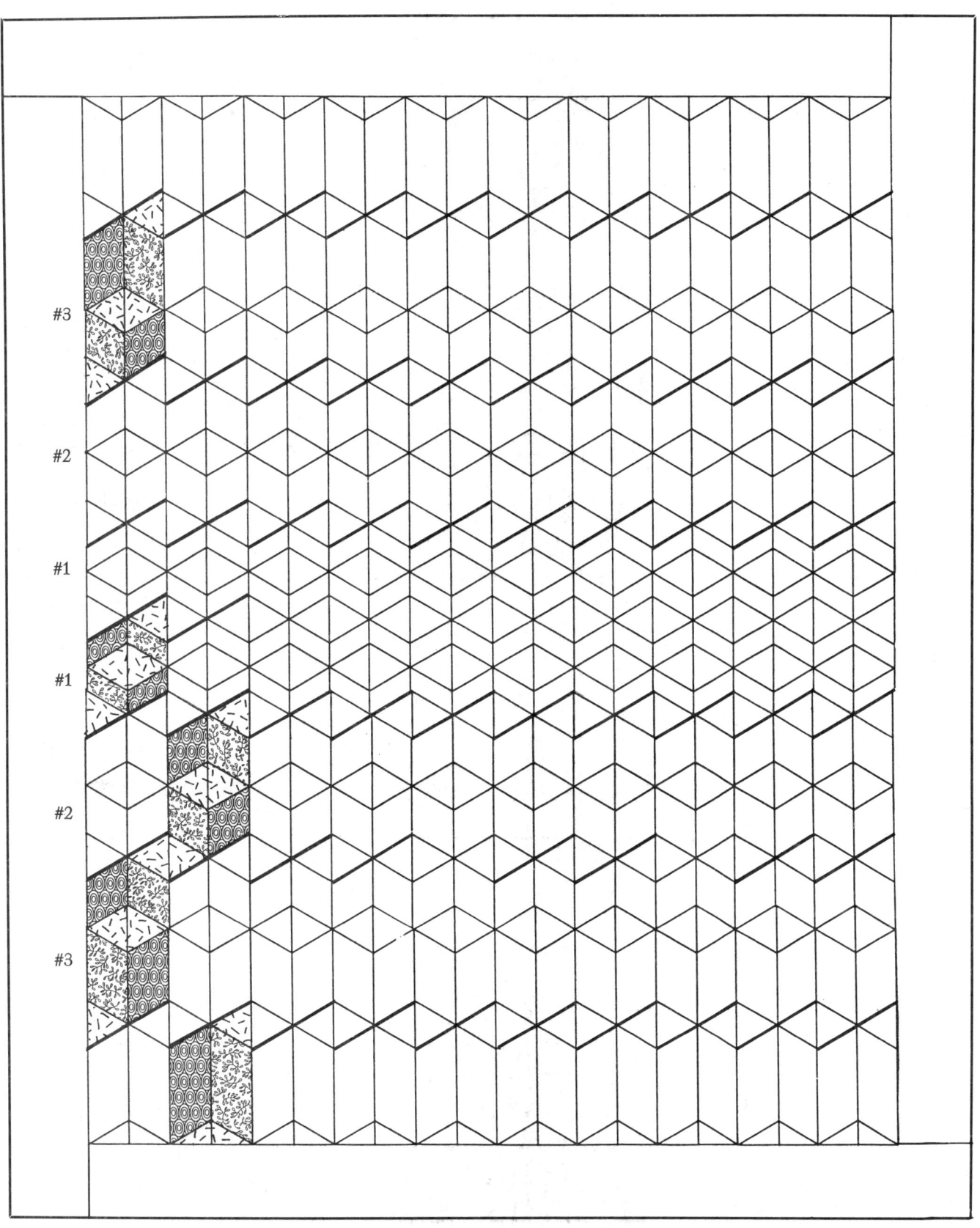

Building Block Quilts 2 – Page fifty-nine

Space Crystal

2½" triangle

Quilt with border: 39½" x 41"

Fabric requirements:

⅓ yd. light fabric
⅓ yd. medium fabric
⅓ yd. dark fabric
⅔ yd. background fabric

Directions:

This design is pieced as a three-sided pattern (see the book Stars and Flowers—Three Sided Patchwork). It is not difficult to piece, but concentrate on getting the proper value in each position.

1. Piece one block of *Tumbling Blocks and Stars*.

Cut: 1 background 6" triangle
      6 light diamonds from 2¼" strip
      6 dark diamonds
      12 medium 2½" triangles
      9 background triangles

Assemble around center 6" triangle according to diagram.

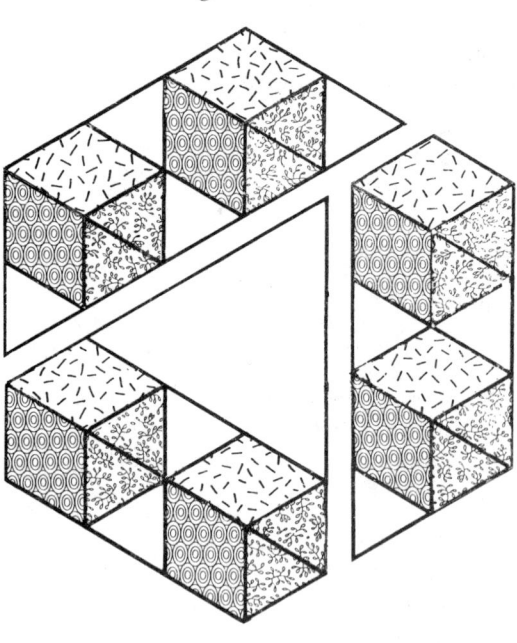
Tumbling Blocks and Stars

2. Piece 6 shaded pyramids according to diagram. Sew 2 half-diamonds (cut from a 2⅝₁₆" strip) together from point to seam allowance and backstitch. Set in the remaining half-diamond. Trim the seam ears off the 3 corners of the triangle, restoring the 60° shape. Piece 6 more shaded pyramids with the medium and light fabrics in reverse position.

3. Sew 3 of #2 to 3 separate sides of #1 according to quilt diagram. This is the center triangle.

4. Construct 6 hexagon-shaped units according to the diagrams below.

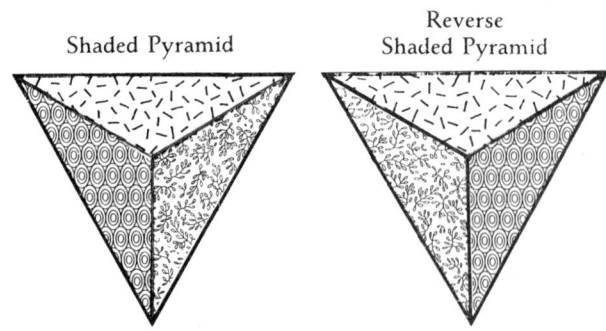
Shaded Pyramid   Reverse Shaded Pyramid

Hex #1

3 dark diamonds from 2¼" strip
2 medium diamonds
3 light diamonds
4 medium triangles
1 light long diamond cut at 4" on the Clearview Triangle
1 dark reverse long diamond
2 background diamonds
2 background flat pyramids cut at 4¼"
2 background diamonds cut from a 4" strip

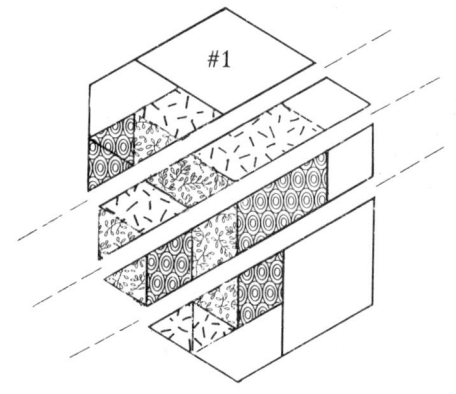

Page sixty — *Building Block Quilts 2*

Space Crystal

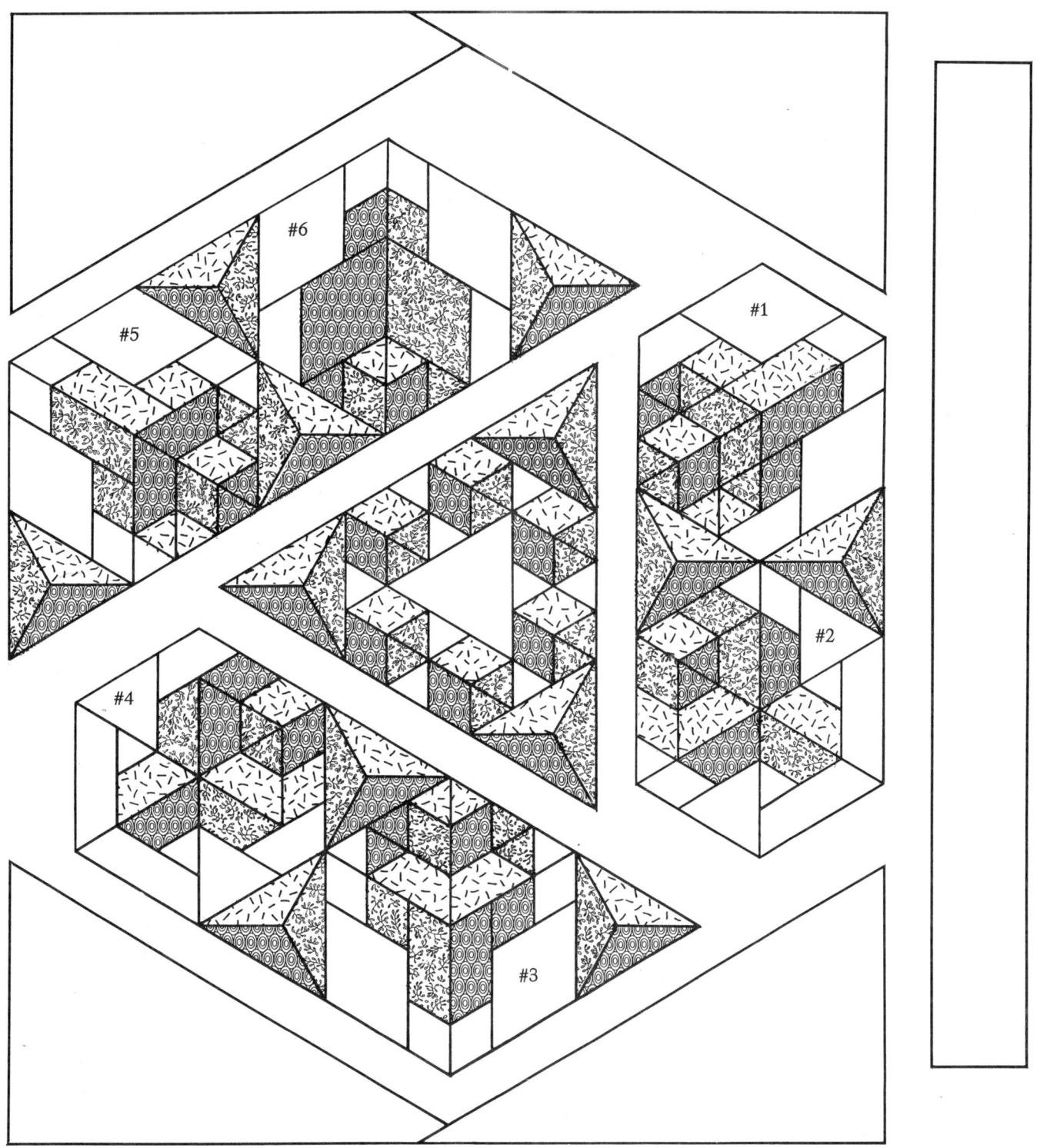

Building Block Quilts 2 – Page sixty-one

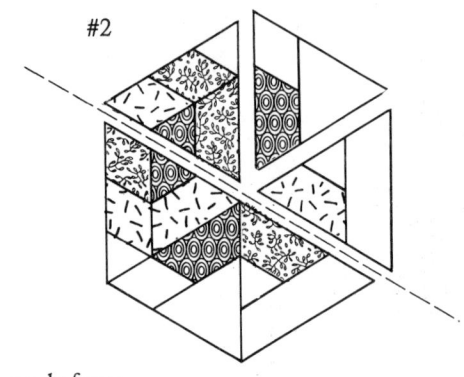

Hex #2

2 medium diamonds from 2¼" strip
2 light diamonds
2 dark triangles
2 dark flat pyramids cut at 4¼" on the Clearview Triangle
2 medium flat pyramids
2 light flat pyramids
4 background triangles
2 background diamonds
2 background 4¼" triangles
2 background flat pyramids cut at 6"

Hex #3

2 dark triangles
2 medium triangles
2 light triangles
2 dark diamonds
2 medium diamonds
2 light flat pyramids cut at 4¼"
1 dark long diamond cut at 4"
1 medium reverse long diamond cut at 4"
2 background triangles
4 background diamonds
2 background 4" diamonds

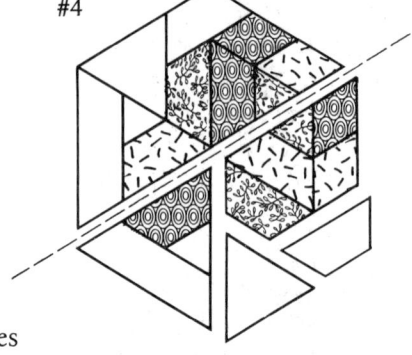

Hex #4

2 dark diamonds
2 light diamonds
2 medium triangles
2 dark flat pyramids cut at 4¼"
2 medium flat pyramids cut at 4¼"
2 light flat pyramids cut at 4¼"
2 background triangles
2 background 4¼" triangles
2 background flat pyramids cut at 4¼"
2 background flat pyramids cut at 6"

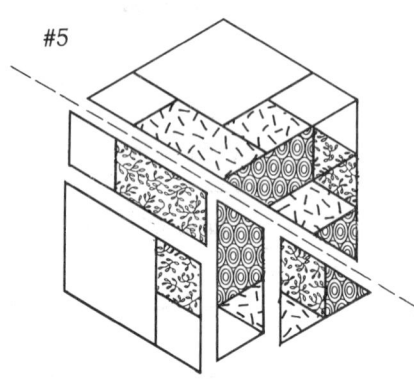

Hex #5

2 dark triangles
2 medium triangles
2 light triangles
2 medium diamonds
2 light diamonds
2 dark flat pyramids cut at 4¼"
1 medium long diamond cut at 4"
1 light reverse long diamond cut at 4"
2 background triangles
4 background diamonds
2 background 4" diamonds

Hex #6

1 dark triangle
1 medium triangle
2 light triangles
2 dark diamonds
2 medium diamonds
1 dark 4" diamond
1 medium 4" diamond
2 background diamonds
2 background flat pyramids
   cut at 4¼"
2 background 4" diamonds

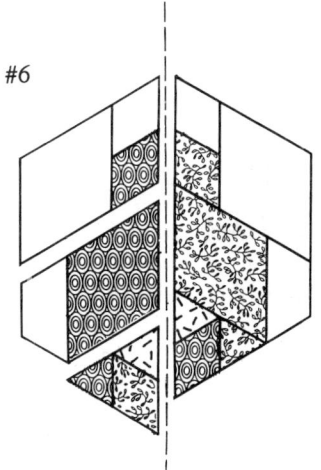

#6

5. Sew a shaded pyramid to Hex #1 and a reverse shaded pyramid to Hex #2 as shown. Sew together. Sew to center triangle.

6. Make another side section from Hex #3, Hex #4, 1 shaded pyramid, and 2 reverse shaded pyramids. Sew to center triangle as shown.

7. Assemble the final side from the remaining Hex units and shaded triangles. Sew on to complete the medallion.

8. To float the medallion, square off with 4 background 21½" half-triangles. Add a 4½" strip of background fabric down each side.

Bibliography

Diehl, Gaston. **Vasarely.** New York: Crown Publishers, Inc., 1973.

Fairfield, Helen. **Patchwork from Mosaics.** London: B.T. Batsford, Ltd., 1985.

Locher, J.L., ed. **The World of M.C. Escher.** New York: Harry N. Abrams, Inc., 1971.

Fisher, Laura. **Quilts of Illusion.** New Jersey: The Main Street Press, 1988.

Gutcheon, Jeffrey. **Diamond Patchwork.** New York: Alchemy Press, 1980.

Locke, John. **Isometric Perspective Designs and How to Create Them.** New York: Dover Publications, Inc., 1981.

Paré, E.G., Loving, R.O., Hill I.L. **Descriptive Geometry.** New York: The Macmillan Company, 1959.

Turner, Harry. **Triad Optical Illusions and How to Design Them.** New York: Dover Publications, Inc., 1983.

Willson. **Mosaic and Tesselated Patterns: How to Create Them.** New York: Dover Publications, Inc., 1983.

Index

Clearview Triangles, pg. 9
Cutting and piecing, pg. 10
    Diamond, cutting, pg. 11
    Diamond, half, cutting, pg. 12
    Flat pyramid, cutting, pg. 11
    Gem shape, cutting, pg. 15
    Half-diamond, sandwich piecing, pg. 16
    Half-triangle, sandwich piecing, pg. 16
    Hexagon, cutting, pg. 14
    Long diamond, cutting, pg. 11
    Long hex, cutting, pg. 15
    Matching triangle, sandwich piecing, pg. 16
    Strips, cutting, pg. 10
    Teardrop, cutting, pg. 13
    Teardrop unit, piecing, pg. 13
    Triangle, cutting, pg. 10
    Triangle half, cutting, pg. 12
Enlarging patterns, pg. 17
Piecing hints, pg. 15
Rules, pg. 10
Shrinking patterns, pg. 17
Triangle size, pg. 10

About the Author

Sara Nephew began her artistry in metalwork. After receiving her B.A. as an Art Major, she worked for a commercial shop, repairing and designing jewelry, and invented a new enamel-on-brass technique. Her cloisonne' work appeared in national exhibits.

She has since turned her interests to quilting, in large part because of the many attractions of fabric. Sara is the originator of a series of tools for rotary cutting isometric shapes, and a nationally known teacher.

Sara is the author of four previous quilting books. ***Quilts from a Different Angle*** was an introduction to 60° triangle quilts. ***My Mother's Quilts: Designs from the Thirties*** helped inspire renewed interest in depression-era quilts. ***Stars and Flowers: Three-Sided Patchwork*** showed how to speed piece 60° quilts with a floral applique appearance. And her fourth book, ***Building Block Quilts,*** explored isometric 3-D illusions.

Sara lives in Snohomish, Washington, with her husband Dale and their three children.

Available from Clearview Triangle

60° 6" Clearview Triangle — ruled every ¼"	$6.50 plus $1.50 shipping*
60° 12" Clearview Triangle — ruled every ¼"	$11.50 plus $2.00 shipping*
60° 8" Mini-Pro — ruled every ⅛"	$9.50 plus $1.75 shipping*
120° Half-Diamond — ruled every ⅛"	$10.50 plus $2.00 shipping*
2-sided Graph Paper — 30 sheets	$5.95 plus $1.00 shipping*

Stars and Flowers: Three-sided Patchwork $12.95 plus $2.00 shipping*
Building Block Quilts $14.95 plus $2.00 shipping*

* Subtract $1.00 from shipping for each item after the first.

ORDER FROM: Clearview Triangle
Dept. 4
8311 180th St. S.E.
Snohomish, WA 98290